Rembrandt and His School: Masterworks from the Frick and Lugt Collections

Rembrandt and His School:
Masterworks from the Frick and Lugt Collections

Colin B. Bailey, Margaret Iacono, Esmée Quodbach,
Louisa Wood Ruby, Joanna Sheers

The Frick Collection
New York

This catalogue is dedicated to the memory of
Melvin R. Seiden (1930–2011), a great friend and
benefactor of The Frick Collection.

Published on the occasion of the exhibition *Rembrandt
and His School: Masterworks from the Frick and Lugt Collections*,
organized by Colin B. Bailey with the assistance of
Margaret Iacono and Joanna Sheers at The Frick
Collection, New York. February 15–May 15, 2011

Authorship of the catalogue is indicated by the authors'
initials: C.B.B., M.I., L.W.R., and J.S.

This publication was organized at The Frick Collection by
Elaine Koss, *Editor in Chief*
Julie Di Filippo, *Assistant Editor*

Design: The Oliphant Press, New York

Principal funding for the exhibition is provided by The
Christian Humann Foundation, Jean-Marie and Elizabeth
Eveillard, and Melvin R. Seiden. Corporate support is
provided by Fiduciary Trust Company International.
The exhibition is also supported by an indemnity from
the Federal Council on the Arts and the Humanities.

The catalogue is made possible by the Robert Lehman
Foundation, Inc. It is also underwritten, in part, by public
funds from the Netherlands Cultural Services and by the
Netherland-America Foundation.

Cover: Rembrandt, *Self-Portrait* (cat. 3)

Frontispiece: Rembrandt, *Self-Portrait, Frowning: Bust*, 1630.
Etching. Fondation Custodia, Collection Frits Lugt, Paris
(Inv. No. 1548)

ISBN 978-0-912114-53-8

Library of Congress Control Number: 2010 942013

FOREWORD

When Henry Clay Frick (1849–1919) was asked whose talents he would most like to possess, he declared, "Rembrandt's." As the largest individual railway stockholder in the world he is also reported to have said that "railways were the Rembrandts of investment." Like Frick, the Dutch art historian Frederik Johannes Lugt (1884–1970) was a great admirer and collector of works by the Dutch artist Rembrandt van Rijn (1606–1669); as a teenager he wrote a biography of the artist, illustrated with his pen and ink copies of Rembrandt's masterpieces.

The Frick Collection begins its 2011 season by presenting Rembrandt's works as seen through the eyes of these two renowned collectors in an exhibition held exclusively in New York between February and May 2011. Five paintings from the permanent collection—four acquired by Frick and the fifth purchased by the Trustees in 1943—are installed together for the first time in the Oval Room. We are particularly grateful to Dorothy Mahon, Conservator in the Sherman Fairchild Center for Paintings Conservation at The Metropolitan Museum of Art for cleaning and conserving the Frick's marvelous *Self-Portrait*. Two of the Frick's paintings—one attributed to a follower of Rembrandt and another by Carel van der Pluym—also underwent treatment at the Metropolitan Museum in preparation for this exhibition.

A complementary display in the Cabinet features ten Rembrandt prints owned by Frick. Additionally, a group of outstanding works on paper from the Lugt Collection, Fondation Custodia, Paris—eleven prints by Rembrandt and fifty-four drawings by the artist and his followers—is on view in our exhibition galleries downstairs. This is an exceptional opportunity for a New York audience to study sheets by the Dutch master with a selection of master drawings from his "circle"—mentors, pupils, fellow artists, and followers—among whom are Ferdinand Bol (1616–1680), Lambert Doomer (1624–1700),

Gerbrand van den Eeckhout (1621–1674), Govert Flinck (1615–1660), Samuel van Hoogstraten (1627–1678), Philips Koninck (1619–1688), Jan Lievens (1607–1674), and Nicolaes Maes (1634–1693). To this group we are adding a single loan of Rembrandt's *Cottage Near the Entrance to a Wood*, 1644, from the Robert Lehman Collection at The Metropolitan Museum of Art. We thank Thomas Campbell, Director, and Dita Amory, Acting Associate Curator-in-Charge of the Robert Lehman Collection, for kindly approving the loan, which will allow visitors to compare the version by Lambert Doomer from the Lugt Collection with Rembrandt's largest drawn landscape.

In early 2009 The Frick Collection had the pleasure of co-organizing *Watteau to Degas: French Drawings from the Frits Lugt Collection*. As the magnificent sheets from this exhibition were deinstalled and packed for their return to Paris, Mària van Berge-Gerbaud, former Director of the Fondation Custodia, and Colin B. Bailey, Associate Director and Peter Jay Sharp Chief Curator at the Frick, discussed the possibility of collaborating again on a future exhibition. Mària van Berge-Gerbaud generously suggested that a selection of the Fondation Custodia's superb collection of drawings and prints by Rembrandt and his circle might be available for loan. Since he was already organizing an exhibition of Rembrandt's works in The Frick Collection, Colin Bailey realized the potential of this extraordinary opportunity, and, in conjunction with his colleagues at the Fondation Custodia, he made the selection of works to be shown in New York. Ger Luijten, who assumed his post as Director of the Fondation Custodia in June 2010, has been steadfast in his support of this collaboration.

Rembrandt and His School coincides with the publication of Peter Schatborn's *Rembrandt and His Circle: Drawings in the Frits Lugt Collection* (2010). This important two-volume work by the former head

of the Rijksprentenkabinet at the Rijksmuseum,
Amsterdam, documents all the Fondation Custodia's
drawings by Rembrandt and his school and is the
definitive catalogue of this collection. We are
immensely grateful to Peter Schatborn for his
assistance and support of our collaboration with
the Fondation Custodia.

This project would not have been possible without
the generous sponsorship of The Christian Humann
Foundation. We also thank Jean-Marie and Elizabeth
Eveillard, Mel Seiden and Janine Luke (in honor of
Colin B. Bailey), and the Fiduciary Trust Company
International for their considerable assistance. To the
Robert Lehman Foundation we are indebted for both
the loan of a drawing by Rembrandt and for their gen-
erous support of this catalogue. We gratefully
acknowledge the support of Barbara Fleischman and
John and Constance Birkelund and offer warmest
thanks to Diane Nixon, the Netherland-America
Foundation, and the Consulate General of the
Kingdom of the Netherlands.

Anne L. Poulet
Director, The Frick Collection

ACKNOWLEDGMENTS

Although Henry Clay Frick and Frits (Frederik) Johannes Lugt were not acquainted, they shared a profound appreciation of art and a generosity of spirit that led them to bequeath their collections to the public. They were also united in their great admiration for the Dutch master Rembrandt van Rijn (1606–1669).

Rembrandt and His School: Masterworks from the Frick and Lugt Collections is the second collaboration between The Frick Collection and the Fondation Custodia. We are grateful for the opportunity to display a group of superb sheets from the Lugt Collection alongside masterworks from the Frick's permanent holdings in an exhibition that unfolds over three spaces at 1 East 70th Street: the Oval Room, the Cabinet, and the downstairs exhibition galleries. Our heartfelt thanks go to our colleagues at the Fondation Custodia, Director Ger Luijten and Mariska de Jonge, Secrétaire/Intendante, and to Mària van Berge-Gerbaud, former Director of the Fondation Custodia.

We recognize several colleagues at The Metropolitan Museum of Art for their support. Above all, we are indebted to the museum's Department of Paintings Conservation, headed by Sherman Fairchild Conservator Michael Gallagher, and in particular to Conservator Dorothy Mahon, for her skillful treatment of the three paintings in our collection mentioned in the Director's Foreword. Nadine Orenstein, Curator of Prints, consulted on the selection of the Frick's works on paper by Rembrandt during the early stages of the exhibition's organization; Dita Amory, Acting Associate Curator-in-Charge of the Robert Lehman Collection, was most supportive of our request to borrow a master drawing from the Lehman Collection.

At The Frick Collection, I wish to thank Anne L. Poulet, Director, for her support and encouragement of this exhibition. Sincerest thanks are due also to Robert Goldsmith, Deputy Director,

Alison Lonshein, General Counsel, Lynne Rutkin, Deputy Director for External Affairs, Rosayn Anderson, Manager of Corporate and Foundation Relations, Heidi Rosenau, Head of Media Relations, and Alexis Light, Media Relations and Marketing Coordinator, for the myriad ways in which they have supported this endeavor.

Diane Farynyk, Registrar and Exhibition Manager, and Allison Galea, Assistant Registrar, oversaw the many details concerning the exhibition's organization. Joseph Godla, Conservator, Adrian Anderson, Senior Galleries Technician, and William Trachet, Senior Conservation Technician, competently handled all aspects of the installation. We are grateful to Stephen Saitas for the installation's elegant design and to Anita Jorgensen for lighting the works to their best advantage.

I was joined in the writing of this catalogue by colleagues from both The Frick Collection and the Frick Art Reference Library, and it is a pleasure to recognize the expertise that we have in house at the Frick: Margaret Iacono, Assistant Curator; Esmée Quodbach, Assistant to the Director of the Center for the History of Collecting in America; Joanna Sheers, Curatorial Assistant; and Louisa Wood Ruby, Head, Photoarchive Research. The catalogue, which builds on, and brings up to date, the scholarship of Bernice Davidson's first volume of *Paintings in The Frick Collection*, published in 1968, could not have been undertaken without the work of Elaine Koss, Editor-in-Chief; Julie Di Filippo, Assistant Editor; and Serena Rattazzi, editorial volunteer, whose patience, efficiency, and expertise are to be commended. Frick Photographer Michael Bodycomb is responsible for much of the beautiful new photography contained herein.

Rika Burnham, Head of Education, and her staff—especially Jennie Coyne, Adrienne Lei, and Viktorya Vilk—were critical in making this exhibition accessible to the general public by implementing

a series of innovative programs. Thanks also go to
Floyd Sweeting, Head of Information Technology
and New Media, Vivian Gill, Web and New Media
Manager, and their staff. I also wish to thank
Ron Gordon and Aaron Tilford of the Oliphant Press
for producing this attractive publication under the
most stringent of deadlines.

I am obliged to several graduate assistants, without
whose organizational and research skills this project
could not have been realized. Above all, I recognize
the contribution of Joanna Sheers, Curatorial
Assistant at The Frick Collection and a doctoral
student at New York University's Institute of Fine
Arts; she has been assisted by Heather Hughes,
doctoral student at the University of Pennsylvania,
and James Lemoine, doctoral student at the Graduate
Center, City University of New York. The staff at the
Frick Art Reference Library greatly assisted in the
production of this catalogue, and we also gratefully
acknowledge the expertise of Sally Brazil, Chief,
Archives and Records Management, and Associate
Archivists Julie Ludwig and Susan Chore for their
help in making available the deep resources of the
Frick Archives.

Colin B. Bailey
Associate Director and Peter Jay Sharp Chief Curator

CONTENTS

Fig. 1. B.L.H. Dabbs (1839–1899), *Henry Clay Frick*, 1898, photograph, Courtesy of The Frick Collection/
Frick Art Reference Library Archives

1. *Henry Clay Frick Collects Rembrandt, 1899–1919*

Esmée Quodbach

Henry Clay Frick (fig. 1) acquired his first Rembrandt, *Portrait of a Young Artist*, in August 1899. At the time, Frick (who was still living at Clayton, his Pittsburgh residence) owned a large number of fashionable contemporary French works—by such artists as Corot, Daubigny, and Breton—plus a handful of minor Old Master pictures. *Portrait of a Young Artist* was not only his first important Old Master but also the first of six paintings to enter Frick's collection under Rembrandt's name (see cat. 4). It depicts an unknown man, presumably an artist, who, with a paintbrush in his right hand, holds a loosely bound sketchbook. The canvas, which bears a false date and signature, probably dates to the 1650s and is now thought to be the work of a Rembrandt pupil or follower.

What sparked Frick's seemingly sudden interest in Rembrandt remains unknown, be it a conversation with a dealer or with one of his artist or collector friends. Competition may well have played a role in Frick's decision to purchase *Portrait of a Young Artist*, and it is probably no coincidence that he acquired his first Rembrandt just five months after his acquaintance A. M. (Alexander McBurney) Byers (1827–1900), the iron manufacturer who was then Pittsburgh's foremost picture collector, had bought his first (alleged) Rembrandt. Around the turn of the twentieth century, the taste for the Dutch School was firmly established in America, and without doubt Rembrandt was its most sought-after artist, as he had been for many years. As early as 1812, three paintings attributed to Rembrandt were included in an exhibition in New York, and over the course of the following decades many more works ascribed to him arrived in the United States.[1] The first authentic Rembrandts most likely only crossed

Fig. 2. Rembrandt, *Portrait of a Man*, c. 1655–60, oil on canvas, 32 7/8 x 25 3/8 inches (83.5 x 64.5 cm), The Metropolitan Museum of Art, New York, Marquand Collection, Gift of Henry G. Marquand, 1890 (91.26.7)

the Atlantic in the 1880s, the decade during which America's newly rich merchant princes began to purchase Europe's Old Masters at an unprecedented rate. The very first autograph Rembrandt to come to the United States may have been *Portrait of a Man* of about 1655–60 (fig. 2), bought by the New York financier Henry G. Marquand (1819–1902) in 1883.[2] (Marquand gave it to The Metropolitan Museum of Art, where it remains to this day.) Before long, a

Rembrandt—often, a series of Rembrandts—was at the top of every aspiring American collector's wish list. When Wilhelm Bode (1845–1929), the distinguished Rembrandt scholar and director of Berlin's Royal Gallery of Paintings, paid his first monthlong visit to the East Coast in the fall of 1893, he already counted thirty authentic Rembrandts there, almost all portraits, the majority of which originated in British and French collections.[3] Dozens of Rembrandts (and so-called Rembrandts) followed in the later years of the Gilded Age.

Nothing is known about the earliest history of Frick's first Rembrandt. Its initial mention dates to 1766, when it was auctioned in Paris as a portrait of the Delft painter "Lenard Bramer" as part of the estate of Jacques-André-Joseph Aved (1702–1766), a well-known portraitist and art dealer. By 1836 it had entered a famed British collection, that of George Howard, the sixth Earl of Carlisle (1773–1848) at Castle Howard in Yorkshire. Some years later, a prominent American traveler, Harriet Beecher Stowe, saw the painting in the Carlisles' London townhouse. "The walls of the drawing-room were beautifully adorned with works of art by the masters," she wrote in 1853. "There was a Rembrandt hanging over the fire-place, which showed finely by the evening light. It was simply a portrait of a man with a broad Flemish hat."[4] The picture was sold by George James Howard, the ninth Earl of Carlisle (1843–1911), in 1897.[5] Why he decided to part with his heirloom remains unknown. Like many of his peers, he may well have been in dire financial straits: scores of British aristocrats chose to sell off artistic treasures— many fine Rembrandts among those—in the late nineteenth century, often in order to save their estates, especially after the unfavorable tax reforms and the introduction of the inheritance tax (death duties) in 1894. In August 1896 the young Bernard Berenson (1865–1959), apparently testing the waters on behalf of Carlisle and his dealer, offered the Rembrandt to Isabella Stewart Gardner (1840–1924), his Boston patron.[6] Berenson vowed that he had never seen a Rembrandt that he had liked so well: here one found "[Rembrandt's] sheer simplicity of supreme genius—no more nor less." The painting was available for what Berenson called "a very reasonable figure," £10,000 (about $50,000)—that is, half of the

exceptional sum of about £20,000 that Mrs. Gardner had paid just two months earlier for her great treasure, Titian's *Rape of Europa*. She soon informed Berenson that she did not have any funds left for the Rembrandt after her purchase of the Titian.

Still for sale, the Carlisle picture was included in the celebrated Rembrandt exhibition (*Rembrandt Tentoonstelling*) at the Stedelijk Museum in Amsterdam in the fall of 1898. With 124 paintings (plus 350 drawings), it was not only the world's first Rembrandt retrospective, but also one of the first "blockbuster" museum exhibitions.[7] "Naturally there is nothing [included in the exhibition] from America, whither some 50 genuine Rembrandts, not to mention a much larger number of spurious ones, have taken flight during the last 20 years," *The Times* of London commented at the time. "But happily these are not, as a rule, of very great importance as compared with the chief pictures here."[8] Among the paintings that caused a stir in Amsterdam were several of Frick's future Rembrandt acquisitions: *The Polish Rider*, then recently rediscovered in a remote castle in Galicia, and the *Old Woman with a Book*, already doubted by some (see cats. 2 and 5). The exhibition also featured the splendid early portrait of the Amsterdam merchant Nicolaes Ruts, which would be purchased by the American financier J. Pierpont Morgan (1837–1913) the following year (see cat. 1, fig. 4). The Trustees of The Frick Collection bought it from Morgan's heirs in 1943.

Although Frick traveled to Europe in the summer of 1898, he returned to the United States before the Amsterdam exhibition opened.[9] (He made multiple trips to Europe yet seems to have visited Holland only once, in 1896.)[10] Frick had probably seen the *Portrait of a Young Artist* sometime before he sailed for Europe in June 1899, at the New York gallery of the London dealer Arthur Tooth. On August 29 of that year he bought the picture from Tooth for $38,000[11]—a sizable sum, albeit $12,000 less than Berenson's asking price some three years earlier. It was the highest amount Frick had paid for a painting until then and just about half of what a total of twenty-five pictures had cost him a few years earlier, in 1895. By comparison, at about the same time Morgan paid £6,000 (roughly $30,000) for *Nicolaes Ruts*, certainly the superior of the two works when

Fig. 3. Attributed to Lewis Stephany, photograph of the *Portrait of a Young Artist*, then attributed to Rembrandt, in situ in the parlor at Clayton, Pittsburgh, Courtesy TFC/FARL Archives

judged by current standards. Frick gave the *Portrait of a Young Artist* a central place in Clayton's parlor (fig. 3).

Not long after Frick had purchased his first Rembrandt, Charles S. Carstairs (1865–1928) of M. Knoedler & Co.—the dealer through whom Frick bought the majority of his paintings—offered his patron another one.[12] The work in question—a "Rembrandt 'Self-Portrait'"—can be identified here as the so-called *Self-Portrait Wearing a Hat and Two Chains* of circa 1640, formerly with the Dukes of Leuchtenberg in Saint Petersburg. After Frick had declined the picture Knoedler sold it to the New York industrialist Herbert L. Terrell (1842–1909).[13] "The Rembrandt is sold [for] $55,000 [a]nd others are likely to go anytime," Carstairs wrote to Frick on November 24, 1900. "I don't suppose you are interested, but if you are, don't delay acquiring masterpieces that would be a glory to any museum." The *Self-Portrait Wearing a Hat and Two Chains* is now in Madrid's Museo Thyssen-Bornemisza, where it is still given to Rembrandt.[14]

In the meantime, the London firm P. & D. Colnaghi had offered Frick another Rembrandt as well, a late portrait of a young woman, supposedly Hendrickje Stoffels (1626–1663), the artist's housekeeper and companion. The painting, which had also been exhibited in Amsterdam in 1898, was "worthy of taking place in your collection by the side of the fine Rembrandt portrait already there," Colnaghi's representative wrote to Frick on November 14, 1900. It belonged to "the last manner of the master, when he produced the most powerful and also the rarest of his works."[15] The picture can be identified here as *Half-Figure of a Young Woman ("Hendrickje Stoffels")* (fig. 4), formerly with the noted Budapest collector Georg von Ráth (1828–1905), many of whose paintings would be sold to Americans. (A few years later, in 1905, Frick would buy another Dutch work from von Ráth's collection, Salomon van Ruysdael's *River Scene*.) Colnaghi's asking price for von Ráth's Rembrandt was £6,000 (or about $30,000). "I do not think I should like to purchase the picture without having a view of it, and should you still have it when I next visit your Country, (which will probably be the middle of next year,) I will be very glad to look at it," Frick informed Colnaghi some two weeks later. "I, however, would not wish you to hold it for me."[16] Another burgeoning Rembrandt collector, the Philadelphia industrialist P.A.B. Widener (1834–1915), refused the painting as well. Unable to find a buyer in America, Colnaghi then took it to Berlin, probably in the hope of selling it to Bode—one of the main competitors of the Americans who was always on the lookout for Rembrandts for his museum—or to one of his many collecting protégés. Soon after, the *"Hendrickje Stoffels"* was indeed bought by a member of Bode's circle.[17] It is now in Frankfurt's Städel Museum, where it is attributed to an unknown pupil of Rembrandt.[18]

In the fall of 1905 the Frick family started renting the former William H. Vanderbilt residence, built in the Greek Revival style and located at 640 Fifth Avenue in New York. The Fricks lived there until 1914, when they moved into their newly built home on Fifth Avenue and East 70th Street. It was during this decade at the Vanderbilt mansion, which boasted an impressive picture gallery, that Frick purchased many of his masterpieces. The ever-worsening economic circumstances of Europe's aristocracy played into the hands of ambitious American collectors such as Frick in the early years of the twentieth century: a veritable exodus of treasures had started, and the international art market was overflowing with great paintings, including some exquisite Rembrandts.

In June 1906 Charles Carstairs told Frick about his negotiations for one of Britain's most illustrious Rembrandts, *The Mill* (fig. 5) in the Lansdowne collection at Bowood, one of the master's rare landscape paintings. "We have been in communication with Lord Lansdowne for about 6 weeks re his wonderful landscape 'The Mill' by Rembrandt," Carstairs wrote from London; "we might possibly get it, but the price would no doubt be $300,000 [about £60,000] . . .—I think the Berlin Museum would buy it even at this price, but the question is before I speak to anyone do you want it? Should I ever get it, I will send a cable immediately. . . ."[19] Apparently, Frick did not have a keen interest in *The Mill*, as he did not answer Carstairs's letter.[20] About two months later, Carstairs briefly mentioned the painting again: "'The Mill' by Rembrandt Lord Lansdowne has refused to sell, we had great hopes of getting it."[21] Again, Frick does not seem to have responded, at least not in writing. His lack of interest in the famous Rembrandt landscape comes as something of a surprise, given his strong inclination for landscapes.

Some four months later, however, on December 31, 1906, Frick bought another cherished "British" Rembrandt from Knoedler, the *Self-Portrait* of 1658 (see cat. 3).[22] Painted two years after the artist's bankruptcy and known as the "Ilchester Rembrandt,"

Fig. 4. Unknown Dutch painter (School of Rembrandt), *Half-Figure of a Young Woman ("Hendrickje Stoffels")*, c. 1660–70, oil on panel, 29 ¼ x 20 ⅛ inches (74.2 x 51.2 cm), Städel Museum, Frankfurt am Main, on loan from the Federal Republic of Germany

it was (and still is) generally considered one of the master's most extraordinary self-portraits. Even the Italophile Berenson, who cared little for the Dutch masters and who mostly thought Rembrandt "overrated," had some good words for it, calling it "one of the crack pictures of that over-admired Dutchman," as he congratulated his patron, Mrs. Gardner, whom he suspected had secretly purchased it.[23] There is also some evidence that Bode may have been interested in buying it for Berlin.[24] Like many acquisitions dating to Frick's "masterpiece years," the *Self-Portrait* came with a prestigious British provenance: since at least

Fig. 5. Rembrandt, *The Mill*, 1645–48, oil on canvas, 34 ½ x 41 ½ inches (87.6 x 105.6 cm), National Gallery of Art, Washington, D.C., Widener Collection, 1942.9.62

1815, when it was exhibited at the British Institution, it had been with the Earls of Ilchester at Melbury Park in Dorset. The picture was again put on display in London in 1889, and in 1899, when it was part of the Rembrandt exhibition at the Royal Academy—Britain's response to Amsterdam's Rembrandt retrospective of the previous year—where it gained much praise.

It was Giles Fox-Strangways, the sixth Earl of Ilchester (1874–1959), who, when confronted with steep taxes after his father's death in 1905, decided to sell his Rembrandt. Initially, his compatriot Roger Fry (1866–1934, fig. 6), who had just been hired by The Metropolitan Museum of Art as its new curator of paintings, tried to broker the sale for Lord Ilchester.[25] In the spring of 1906, Fry brought the *Self-Portrait* to the attention of J. Pierpont Morgan, then the Metropolitan's president, for purchase by his institution for £30,000 (about $150,000). A connoisseur, critic, and painter, Fry was involved in a number of sales to Americans of highly important pictures from esteemed British collections—for example, he later helped Frick with Holbein's *Sir Thomas More* (bought in 1912) and Van Dyck's *James, Seventh Earl of Derby, His Lady and Child* (bought in 1913). Paradoxically, Fry was also a founder of Britain's National Art-Collections Fund, established in 1903 to save major works of art for the nation. One cannot help but wonder how he reconciled the Fund's patriotic mission with the (sometimes aggressive) initiatives he took privately to sell his country's artistic heritage abroad.

Fig. 6. A. C. Cooper, *Roger Fry*, February 28, 1918, sepia-toned vintage print, 7 ¾ in. x 5 ⅞ inches (19.8 x 15 cm), National Portrait Gallery, London, Purchased, 1979, NPG x13109.

At first, Morgan told Fry he thought the asking price for the Rembrandt *Self-Portrait* too high; a lower bid on his behalf was refused by Lord Ilchester. When Morgan changed his mind, his decision came too late: an impatient Ilchester had shown the picture to Carstairs and his sometime partner, Colnaghi's Otto Gutekunst. "Just Concluded purchase greatest Rembrandt portrait of Himself existing," a triumphant Carstairs cabled to Frick on November 5, 1906.[26] Still, it was only after weeks of complicated negotiations that Frick bought the *Self-Portrait*—for a high price, $225,000 (about £45,000), minus a credit of $25,000 for a painting by the once-coveted Jules

Breton.[27] The majestic Rembrandt was hung in the Gallery at 640 Fifth Avenue, where all of Frick's Rembrandts would reside. "I am delighted you are so pleased with the great Rembrandt, it will always be a great joy to you & we were all very lucky to have it," Carstairs wrote to Frick in February 1907.[28] The picture became one of Frick's personal favorites, together with Bellini's *St. Francis in the Desert*, Holbein's *Sir Thomas More*, Vermeer's *Mistress and Maid*, and his third Rembrandt, *The Polish Rider*.[29]

In the fall of 1909 Frick contributed eight Dutch paintings, including the Ilchester *Self-Portrait* and *Portrait of a Young Artist*, to the so-called Hudson-Fulton Celebration at the Metropolitan Museum, America's first grand showcase of its holdings of seventeenth-century Dutch art.[30] The exhibition, at least as ambitious as it was successful, was organized by the Metropolitan's new curator of decorative arts, the young Wilhelm (William) Valentiner (1880–1958), a German Rembrandt scholar, a protégé of Bode's, and a major influence on American collectors (and museums) for decades to come. Almost all of the East Coast's great collectors of Old Masters participated—including, besides Frick, Widener, Morgan, the New York department store magnate Benjamin Altman (1840–1913), and Louisine Havemeyer (1858–1929), widow of the New York sugar tycoon Henry Havemeyer (1847–1907). Rembrandt was the undeniable star of the Hudson-Fulton Celebration. Out of a total of 149 Dutch paintings, no fewer than 37 Rembrandts were on view, albeit a jumble of authentic and alleged works by current standards.[31] (In addition, there were 21 Halses, 12 works by Jacob van Ruisdael, 11 Cuyps, and, impressively, 6 of America's 7 Vermeers.) Remarkably, almost all of the Hudson-Fulton's Rembrandts were portraits, in addition to just a handful of history pictures. According to Valentiner, who, through his contacts with scholars, collectors, and dealers on both sides of the Atlantic, had an excellent sense of the most recent wanderings of Rembrandt's pictures, the selection on view at the Metropolitan represented just over one-half of the seventy Rembrandts that were in America by this time.[32] In a review of the exhibition, Claude Phillips, Keeper of The Wallace Collection and one of Roger Fry's co-founders of the National Art-Collections Fund, mourned the recent sale of the Ilchester *Self-Portrait*, which, as he wrote, was "the greatest treasure" of all the paintings on view, as well as "the most irreparable loss to England." Moreover, Phillips thought the picture was "the crowning glory" of Frick's collection."[33]

The Rembrandt craze continued, although certain kinds of paintings fared much better than others on the market: America's chief collectors had a distinct preference for Rembrandt's portraits and self-portraits, and little or no interest in his religious scenes. In 1909, for example, Frick, Widener, Morgan, and Altman all refused *The Descent from the Cross* (now in the National Gallery of Art, Washington, D.C.) because of its religious subject, according to *The New York Times*.[34] Still, they willingly paid ever higher prices for many other Rembrandts. On April 15, 1910, Roger Fry cabled Frick that *The Polish Rider*, one of the world's most sought-after Rembrandts, was on offer for £60,000 (about $300,000).[35] The mysterious equestrian scene—one of two in Rembrandt's oeuvre—was still with the Tarnowski family at Castle Dzików (fig. 7) in an isolated part of Galicia, near the Russian border, where it had been since 1834 and where the Dutch Rembrandt scholar Abraham Bredius (1855–1946) had rediscovered it in 1897.[36] The story of the rediscovery, first published by Bredius in a Dutch journal, was well known: when Bredius got to the castle, he gained permission to view the collection, which included, as he reported, "among a great deal of trash" a few fine pictures.[37] As for the *The Polish Rider*—then known as the "Lisowczyk" ("Soldier of the Lisowski regiment")—"just one glance, and a few

seconds' study of its technique" were enough to convince Bredius that here, "in this remote outpost," hung "one of Rembrandt's greatest masterpieces!" Without delay, Bredius, then director of the Mauritshuis in The Hague, tried to persuade the painting's owner, Count Zdzisław Tarnowski (1862–1937), to sell his Rembrandt to the Dutch state—to no avail. "And such a delicious work has to remain hanging for how much longer at a faraway, almost inaccessible castle in Galicia?" Bredius complained. Yet at least Tarnowski agreed to lend the pearl of his collection to the upcoming Rembrandt exhibition in Amsterdam: the following year, it was one of the highlights there, and it also received the name under which it is known today.[38] After the exhibition, Tarnowski received many offers for his

Fig. 7. Castle Dzików, near Tarnobrzeg, Poland, probably early 20th century

Rembrandt—from Brussels, Paris, Berlin, and Holland, according to one source, which does not mention any interest from the United States. Nonetheless, for years, Tarnowski allegedly "repelled the overtures of dealers" by placing "an almost prohibitive price" on the work.[39]

It was not until the spring of 1910 that Tarnowski was willing to part with *The Polish Rider*. A nationalist, he apparently sold his painting in order to be able to acquire a large tract of beautiful forest that bordered on his estate, thus preventing it from falling into foreign hands.[40] Shortly after Fry had cabled that

The Polish Rider was on the market, Frick asked him to buy the picture at once, provided its condition was good, and at a lower price if possible: "You have authority to do as you think best in all matters."[41] Later, Fry described to a friend how he had traveled to Castle Dzików —a journey of two and a half days—to inspect the Rembrandt. Fry, as his friend told the story, arrived in the isolated castle, full of second-rate French furniture and 1880s objects, convinced—much like Bredius some thirteen years earlier—that it was "impossible" that "any real work of art" could exist in such dismal surroundings.[42] "[A]nd then, suddenly, a cord was pulled, a curtain was rolled back, and there, before [Fry's] eyes, was revealed one of the world's masterpieces of painting—*The Polish Rider*." Fry purchased the work on behalf of Frick for Tarnowski's asking price, a dear £60,000 (about $300,000).[43] "Enchanted," Frick cabled to his envoy when he received *The Polish Rider* that summer.[44]

Frick added two other Rembrandts to his collection in 1910, albeit merely temporarily. On December 31 he paid Knoedler $175,000 for two early pendants on panel, *Portrait of a Bearded Man in a Wide-Brimmed Hat, possibly Pieter Sijen* of 1633 and *Portrait of a Forty-Year-Old Woman, possibly Marretje Cornelisdr. van Grotewal* of 1634 (figs. 8 and 9), both formerly with the Earl of Beauchamp. Within a year, Frick returned the pair, for a credit of $175,000, which was then taken as a first payment for Johannes Vermeer's *Officer and a Laughing Girl*, which he purchased shortly after.[45] Why Frick sent the two crisply painted Rembrandts back is not clear. Of course, he may simply have preferred Rembrandt's later style. Not long after Frick had traded the Beauchamp pendants, Knoedler sold them to one of his business partners, the New York financier William H. Moore. After Moore's death in 1922, the Rembrandts remained with his widow and then with their son until 1960, when they were sold

Fig. 8. Rembrandt, *Portrait of a Bearded Man in a Wide-Brimmed Hat, possibly Pieter Sijen*, 1633, oil on panel, 27 ½ x 21 ½ inches (69.9 x 54.6 cm), Norton Simon Art Foundation, Pasadena, M.1977.31.P

at Sotheby's in London. Subsequently, the pendants each went their separate ways. *Portrait of a Bearded Man in a Wide-Brimmed Hat* is now in the Norton Simon Art Foundation in Pasadena, while *Portrait of a Forty-Year-Old Woman* is in the J. B. Speed Art Museum in Louisville.

The year 1911 was one of the best for the sale of Old Masters in the United States. In April, P.A.B. Widener bought Lord Lansdowne's *Mill* (see fig. 5) for £100,000 (about $500,000), thereby setting a new record. Weeks earlier, when the sale was still under negotiation, it had been noted in the press that even

Fig. 9. Rembrandt, *Portrait of a Forty-Year-Old Woman, possibly Marretje Cornelisdr. van Grotewal*, 1634, oil on panel, 27 ⁷/₁₆ x 22 inches (69.7 x 55.9 cm), Collection of the Speed Art Museum, Louisville, Purchased with funds contributed by individuals, corporations, and the entire community of Louisville, as well as the Commonwealth of Kentucky, 1977.16

though the identity of *The Mill*'s prospective buyer was concealed under the vague declaration "an American," Frick's name was freely mentioned in "well-informed quarters."[46] By a process of elimination, the British newspapers had suggested that only three Americans were likely to give as much as £100,000 for a painting such as this one: Frick, Widener, and Altman. When asked, all three had denied they intended to purchase the Rembrandt.

Perhaps as a result of the spectacular sale of

The Mill and, furthermore, of the fact that the press had identified him as a leading American collector with a bottomless purse, Frick received at least six offers of Rembrandts in 1911. Four were proposed to him in quick succession in the spring: a purported portrait of the master's wife, Saskia (1612–1642), in a Swiss collection; a "picture of a Rabbi" with Count Nostitz of Prague; an unnamed work in the possession of a Baron von Olegar in London—"certainly in every respect equal to [the Lansdowne *Mill*]," Olegar boasted; and, lastly, an unnamed painting in an unidentified collection in Saint Petersburg, Russia.[47] Frick rejected all four.[48] Subsequently, in July 1911, Roger Fry—who had also brought the Nostitz picture to Frick's attention—informed Frick that the Earl of Denbigh's Rembrandt, a late biblical scene, *Hagar and Ishmael Taking Leave of Abraham* of circa 1650, was for sale for £35,000 (about $175,000).[49] Once again, Frick showed no interest; not only was the painting's subject religious, but, as he could well have known, it was already disputed at the time. "I do not wish to purchase anything unless it ranks with the Rembrandts I have and the Velasquez [*sic*]. So you see my standard is now so high it is not likely I will soon add any pictures to my collection," Frick wrote to Fry on July 31, 1911.[50] *Hagar and Ishmael Taking Leave of Abraham* is now in the M. H. de Young Memorial Museum, San Francisco, where it is attributed to Barent Fabritius (1624–1673).

Yet another British Rembrandt, the Earl of Feversham's so-called *Dutch Merchant*, a late portrait, was offered to Frick in October 1911. "I need hardly say it is a far finer & more covetable picture than "The Mill," Feversham's middleman wrote.[51] The owner asked a considerable £80,000 (about $400,000) for his heirloom, which had been well received when it was part of London's Rembrandt exhibition in 1899. This time Frick did indeed show an interest, asking Fry to inspect the painting on his behalf. "You would not regret getting it," Fry wrote after he had seen it. "It is undoubtedly a masterpiece and one that everyone would recognize as such. I only mean that it does not touch the highest notes of Rembrandt's imagination. . . . It is not so fine as your Ilchester portrait."[52]

Soon after, Frick informed Fry that at present he did not wish to purchase the "Dutch Merchant."[53] "Cannot decide about Rembrandt without seeing the picture," he cabled Feversham's go-between on November 14, 1911.[54] Some five months later, when Frick saw it in London—by then its price had dropped by more than one-third to £50,000 (about $250,000)—he declined it once again.[55] Nevertheless, on May 4, 1912, *The New York Times* mistakenly reported that Frick had bought it.[56] Currently known as *Portrait of a Man with a Letter* and given to a follower of Rembrandt by most scholars, it is part of the Rothschild collection at the Château de Pregny, Switzerland.

Wilhelm Bode, on his recent visit to the United States, had declared that in ten or twenty years the country would possess the finest body of Rembrandt's works outside of the Hermitage, *The New York Times* wrote on December 31, 1911.[57] A very considerable number of these pictures originated in English collections, the newspaper noted, adding that there were now eighty-two authentic Rembrandts in the United States, twelve of which had been acquired since the Hudson-Fulton Celebration. The English nation assumed a certain degree of fixity for these proud possessions, and it was not considered possible that they could be mobilized and marched out of the country to attack the aesthetic sensibilities of America, the article's author argued: "But, as a matter of fact, they are marching out at a tremendous rate of speed and nothing is less probable than that they will ever return to England."

Frick received yet more Rembrandt offers. In the summer of 1912 an intermediary for the Anglo-Irish dealer and collector Sir Hugh Lane (1875–1915) tried to interest Frick in the early *Portrait of a Lady with a Glove*, then also known as The Demidoff Rembrandt.[58] No written evidence of Lane's or his intermediary's attempts remains in the Frick Archives; their interactions with Frick, if any, were probably only verbal, and may have taken place through a go-between, such as Carstairs. Nevertheless, Lane's frustration is clear

from his correspondence with his aunt, the Irish dramatist Lady Augusta Gregory (1852–1932), who had encouraged him to court American collectors. "If Frick does not write I will hardly be disappointed," Lane wrote to Lady Gregory on August 8, 1912. "Every picture buyer gets so many offers of this kind that nothing less than a good talk would awaken a real desire to see the picture."[59] "I did not like the American collectors," Lane wrote later, after his first visit to America.[60] He sold the portrait to the South African financier Max Michaelis (1852–1932). When Michaelis exhibited it in London in 1913 as the masterpiece of his collection, doubt was cast on its attribution to Rembrandt. Lane took the work back and bequeathed it to the National Gallery of Ireland in Dublin instead. It is now attributed to Rembrandt's studio, c. 1632–33.[61] In the spring of 1915, however, Frick purchased two key works from Lane's collection, Holbein's *Thomas Cromwell* and Titian's *Portrait of a Man in a Red Cap*. Unfortunately, Lane would not live to celebrate this success. Still in the midst of his dealings with Frick, he died on May 7, 1915, aboard the RMS *Lusitania*, after the vessel had been torpedoed by the German navy. Ten days later, Frick authorized his bank to remit £60,000— his payment for the Holbein and the Titian—to Lane's estate.[62]

A major late Rembrandt, *Lucretia* of 1664 (fig. 10), was auctioned in New York as part of the estate sale of the textile magnate Matthew C. D. Borden (1842–1912) in February 1913. The painting—a dramatic portrayal of the virtuous Roman matron Lucretia, about to stab herself in the heart—was bought by Knoedler for $130,000—the highest price of the sale.[63] Interestingly, Knoedler was unable to find an American buyer for the superb yet gruesome Rembrandt. According to Abraham Bredius, who had visited Frick in November of that year at Eagle Rock, his "cottage" in Pride's Crossing, Massachusetts, Frick "found the subject so unpleasant that he was simply not interested."[64] Benjamin Altman and Mrs. (Maria Antoinette) Evans of Boston had turned the *Lucretia* down for the same reason, Bredius noted, "so that the piece had become unsaleable here!"[65] To date, no evidence of Knoedler's offer or Frick's alleged negative response has been found in the Frick Archives. Even so, it is not unlikely that Knoedler gave Frick, as its best client, the right of first refusal of *Lucretia*, and Frick may well have explained his aversion to the picture to Bredius. Whatever the case, *Lucretia* was purchased later in 1913 by a Dutch dealer; it was one of just a few Rembrandts to make it back to Holland after having been brought over to the United States. From Holland, however, the painting soon left for Denmark, only to return to the States once again when Knoedler bought it in 1921. Subsequently, it was purchased by Frick's best friend, Andrew Mellon (1855–1937), founder of Washington's National Gallery of Art. Mellon left *Lucretia* to "his" institution, where it remains today.

Another exceptional late Rembrandt, *Portrait of a Boy* (fig. 11), long thought to be a portrait of the artist's son, Titus (1641–1668), was brought to Frick's attention in May 1914, notably by his interior decorator Sir Charles Allom (1865–1947). "I have some very interesting news from Lord Spencer," Allom wrote from London. "He is after all willing to consider the sale of his famous Rembrandt 'Titus,' and you could go see it on your return from Paris, if you would like to."[66] Once again, no written response from Frick is known; whether he was interested or not in the portrait, then in the renowned Spencer collection at Althorp, remains unclear. Still, of all the Rembrandts that Frick could perhaps have bought, one wishes that he would have pursued this one, both lovely and magnificent. Lord Spencer sold the picture in October 1915, for an approximate £35,000 (about $175,000), but to whom was not immediately apparent.[67] For a few days Frick was once again a prime suspect, until he

Fig. 10. Rembrandt, *Lucretia*, 1664, oil on canvas, 47 ¼ x 39 ¼ inches (120 x 101 cm), National Gallery of Art, Washington, D.C., Andrew W. Mellon Collection, 1937.1.76

"flatly denied" the rumor to *The New York Times*.[68] The buyer, as it soon turned out, was the British collector Sir Herbert Cook (1868–1939)—one of Fry's co-founders of the National Art-Collections Fund. "Rembrandt Not for Us," *The New York Times* announced on November 30, 1915.

Frick received more offers of Rembrandt paintings in the later 1910s, not all of which can be mentioned here.[69] The last picture he bought under the master's name was *Old Woman with a Book*, once thought to be Rembrandt's mother (see cat. 5). Nothing is certain about the painting's earliest history. By the early 1780s, however, it was recorded as being with Pilaer

Fig. 11. Rembrandt, *Portrait of a Boy*, 1655–60, oil on canvas, 25 ½ x 22 inches (64.8 x 55.9 cm), The Norton Simon Foundation, Pasadena, F.1965.2.P

and Beeckmans, dealers in Antwerp. John Adams (1735–1826), then the United States first Minister Plenipotentiary to Holland, paid their collection a visit in 1782 and probably saw *Old Woman with a Book* there. "The most remarkable piece in this collection is an old woman, his mother, with a bible on the table before her, by Rembrandt," Adams noted in his diary on October 21. "This is called his master-piece; it is indeed an admirable picture."[70] Adams, who may have been the first American to write, however briefly, about a (purported) Rembrandt, may have remembered incorrectly that there was a "table" before the old woman. (In the Frick painting, the Bible rests in the woman's lap.) Still, it is possible that the Antwerp

dealers showed Adams a different Rembrandt with the same theme in their possession.

Frick acquired *Old Woman with a Book*, then most recently with the Paris mining magnate Jules Porgès (1829–1921), in May 1916 through the dealer Edward Brandus for a steep 1,200,000 francs (about $200,000).[71] At the time, Frick was not aware of the fact that Bode, Bredius, and several others no longer accepted it as autograph. Indeed, Brandus had declared in writing that the painting was "guaranteed by Bredius, Bode, Hofstede de Groot, Friedlander and Valentiner"—all the noted Rembrandt experts of the day.[72] It was Bredius himself who brought the painting's demotion to Frick's attention a few months after he had purchased it, informing the collector that it had been reattributed to a minor Dutch painter, Carel van der Pluym (1625–1672), and urging him to "try to give it back!"[73] Frick, however, was unwilling to accept the picture's deattribution and chose not to part with the picture. (For further details regarding the ensuing controversy, see cat. 5.) Today, *Old Woman with a Book* is generally accepted as a work by Van der Pluym, who probably studied under Rembrandt between 1645 and 1648. The painting most likely dates to the mid-1650s.

The American art market changed significantly in the later 1910s. Several of the country's foremost collectors died: Morgan and Altman in 1913; Widener in 1915; and John G. Johnson in 1917. Other factors contributed as well, chief among these the establishment of a federal income tax in 1913 and, even more important, the outbreak of World War I, which all but paralyzed the international art trade. "I really doubt the wisdom of making a purchase of pictures at this

time, and do so rather reluc-
tantly," Frick wrote to Carstairs
in December 1914. "It is most
difficult to tell what the future
has in store for us, and at
present it seems to me that
pictures will decline rather than
advance in value."[74] Perhaps it
was with this uncertainty in
mind that Frick had bought
three Rembrandt drawings from
Knoedler in the previous year:
two landscapes and, notably, an
Old Testament scene, whose
prices (ranging from about
$3,000 to $6,300) were a mere
fraction of the sums he had paid
for Rembrandt's paintings.[75]
According to the inventories of
Frick's Manhattan residence at the time of his death,
the drawings were displayed in the Sitting Room
Vestibule on the mansion's second floor.[76] Frick also
purchased Rembrandt etchings from Knoedler in the
final years of his collecting career: *The Three Trees* and
The Goldweigher's Field in 1915 (see section IV), plus
three other landscapes, two portraits, and *St. Francis
beneath a Tree Praying* in 1916. At $6,000 the famed
Three Trees was the most expensive of these; the
cheapest was, at $1,650, *Cottage with the White Paling*.[77]
According to the inventories, these etchings were
all hung in the North Corridor of the second floor
of the residence.

Frick made his last Rembrandt purchases less than
a month before his unexpected death on December 2,
1919. On November 3 he bought another three
etchings from Knoedler, notably all three scenes
from the life of Christ.[78] After his death, two of
these—*Christ Presented to the People (Ecce Homo)*
and *Christ Crucified between Two Thieves ("The Three
Crosses")*—were hung in the 70th Street vestibule
of the residence; the third, *Christ Healing the Sick
(The Hundred Guilder Print)* (see section III), was
displayed in the Stair Hall, according to the above-
mentioned inventories. It appears that these etchings
were in fact the last works of art invoiced to Frick
during his lifetime.

At his death, Frick's collection—one of the richest

Fig. 12. Photograph of the West Gallery of the Frick residence
(now The Frick Collection) at 1 East 70th Street, New York,
1927, Courtesy of The Frick Collection/Frick Art Reference
Library Archives

of America's Gilded Age—was bequeathed to the
public (fig. 12). "The late Henry C. Frick was one of
the small group of American collectors of art whose
collecting was done with the mingling of personal
ardor and sound judgment essential to success in
this very difficult pursuit," wrote *The New York Times*
on December 7, 1919. "When Henry Frick the steel
magnate is but dimly remembered, Henry Frick the
art collector will live in the thought of the people."[79]

*I wish to thank Colin B. Bailey, Margaret Iacono,
Edgar Munhall, Inge Reist, Louisa Wood Ruby,
and Joanna Sheers, all at The Frick Collection and
Frick Art Reference Library, for their help and their
insightful comments on this essay. I am also most grateful
to Sally Brazil, Susan Chore, and Julie Ludwig of the
Frick Art Reference Library Archives.*

NOTES

1   See New York 1812, respectively, *Portrait of a Dutch
    Lady* (cat. no. 12); *Portrait of a Dutch Counsellor* (cat. no.
    18); *The Head of Isaac (A Study)* (cat. no. 142). The

present whereabouts of these works are unknown.

2   The portrait is still generally considered to be by Rembrandt, although its condition hampers the decision on its attribution.

3   "Criticised by an Expert; Dr. Wilhelm Bode Talks about Art in This Country," in *The New York Times*, October 11, 1893, p. 1.

4   Stowe 1854, Letter XIV ("Dinner with the Earl of Carlisle"), London, May 2 [1853], p. 131. George William Frederick Howard, the seventh Earl of Carlisle (1802–1864), wrote a preface for Stowe's *Uncle Tom's Cabin* (1852).

5   The ninth Earl, who sold many works from his family's collection, was also the previous owner of Sir Anthony Van Dyck's *Frans Snyders*, bought by Frick in 1909 for $200,000.

6   For Berenson's offer and Gardner's response, see Hadley 1987, pp. 61–64.

7   See van Thiel 1992, pp. 11–93.

8   "The Rembrandt Exhibition at Amsterdam," in *The [London] Times*, September 9, 1898, p. 2.

9   Frick sailed from New York to Liverpool on June 22 and returned on August 3, 1898.

10 An itinerary (possibly in Mrs. Frick's hand) from 1896 records a stay in The Hague; see Helen Clay Frick Papers, Series: Travel (Scrapbook of memorabilia, 1887–1922), The Frick Collection/Frick Art Reference Library Archives (hereafter: TFC/FARL Archives).

11 See Henry Clay Frick Papers, Series II: Correspondence (Arthur Tooth & Sons), TFC/FARL Archives. Frick sailed from New York (to Cherbourg?) on June 6 and returned on August 29, 1899, the day he bought the painting from Tooth. For the price, see *Paintings and Other Works of Art Owned by Henry C. Frick* (Red Book), folio 49, Henry Clay Frick Art Collection Files, TFC/FARL Archives.

12 For the offer, as mentioned in material in the Knoedler & Company Archives, New York (currently closed), and for the quotation below from the letter by Carstairs, see Saltzman 2008, pp. 169–70. To date, no material regarding this offer has been located in the TFC/FARL Archives.

13 According to notes by Cynthia Saltzman, based on material in the Knoedler & Company Archives. I would like to thank Ms. Saltzman for making this information available to me.

14 The attribution is no longer universally accepted.

15 P. & D. Colnaghi & Co., London, to Frick, November 14, 1900, Henry Clay Frick Papers, Series II: Correspondence (P. & D. Colnaghi & Co.), TFC/FARL Archives. Also see Colnaghi's follow-up letter to Frick, dated November 16, 1900, same location. Part of the letter (there attributed to Colnaghi's Edmond F. Deprez) is also cited in Hall 1992, p. 15, where no date is mentioned. For the offer, see also Howard 2010, p. 16, and Saltzman 2008, p. 33. The Rembrandt is not identified in these sources.

16 Frick to P. & D. Colnaghi & Co., London, November 27, 1900, Henry Clay Frick Papers, Series: Letterpress Books, vol. 18, p. 471, TFC/FARL Archives.

17 By 1905 the work was recorded in the collection of the Berlin banker Robert von Mendelssohn (1857–1917), who had probably bought it a few years earlier.

18 See Krempel 2005, pp. 144–50, as "Dutch Painter (School of Rembrandt), c. 1660–70."

19 Carstairs to Frick, June 18, 1906, Henry Clay Frick Papers, Series II: Correspondence (Charles S. Carstairs), TFC/FARL Archives.

20 A penciled notation in Frick's hand at the top of the letter (see previous note) reads: "Not Ans'd, File." The next outgoing letter from Frick to Carstairs is dated October 12, 1906, and concerns paintings by Reynolds, Corot, and Maris.

21 Carstairs to Frick, August 12, 1906, Henry Clay Frick Art Collection Files, Series I: Purchases (Corot, Jean-Baptiste Camille, *Le Lac* [*The Lake*]), TFC/FARL Archives.

22 For a case study of Frick's acquisition of the *Self-Portrait*, see Saltzman 2008, pp. 180–96. See also pp. 32–36 in Howard 2010.

23 Berenson to Gardner, undated letter [1906]; see Hadley 1987, p. 388.

24 See Saltzman 2010, p. 191.

25 For Fry's involvement, see Sutton 1985, pp. 139–40, 154, letters nos. 8–11.

26 Carstairs to Frick, November 5, 1906, Henry Clay Frick Papers, Series II: Correspondence (Carstairs, Charles S.), TFC/FARL Archives. The cable is reprinted in Saltzman 2008, p. 181.

27 For the price, see Bill Book No. 2, p. 39, Henry Clay Frick Art Collection Files, TFC/FARL Archives. The Breton, *Last Gleanings*, is now in the Henry E. Huntington Library and Art Galleries, San Marino, California.

28 Carstairs to Frick, February 18, 1907, Henry Clay Frick Papers, Series II: Correspondence (Carstairs, Charles S.), TFC/FARL Archives.

29 Frick's favorites are listed in Harvey 1928, pp. 335–36.

30 See Valentiner 1909, vol. 2.

31 For the Rembrandts, see ibid., cat. nos. 74–107, 104B, 107A-B.

32 See ibid., "Preface," p. ix.

33 Claude Phillips, *New York Evening Post*, November 13, 1909, p. 5, as cited in Minty 2003, p. 248.

34 See "The $500,000 Rembrandt," in *The New York Times*, September 17, 1922, where it is also mentioned that in 1909 "some doubt was . . . entertained whether it was a genuine Rembrandt." No evidence of the offer to Frick has as yet been found in the Frick Archives. *The Descent from the Cross*, then with Kleinberger Galleries, was initially taken back to Europe. Ironically, it was bought in 1921 by Widener's son, Joseph, who left it to the National Gallery of Art. It is now attributed to a member of Rembrandt's workshop, probably Constantijn van Renesse (1626–1680).

35 Fry to Frick, April 15, 1910, Henry Clay Frick Art Collection Files, Series I: Purchases (Rembrandt Harmensz. van Rijn, *The Polish Rider*, Folder 1 of 4), TFC/FARL Archives. For this acquisition, see also Bailey 2002, pp. 10–12.

36 For the work's earlier provenance, see cat. 2. Rembrandt's only other equestrian scene, *Portrait of Frederick Rihel on Horseback*, probably painted in 1663, is in the The National Gallery, London.

37 Bredius 1897, pp. 197–99, where it is noted that the painting was already known to Bode and Émile Michel. The quotations in this paragraph (translated by this author) have been taken from this article.

38 The name was given by Cornelis Hofstede de Groot, as noted in Held 1944, p. 250.

39 As noted in *The New York Times*, May 15, 1910, p. SM15, quoting from the *Morning Post* of London. I have not been able to identify any interested parties besides Bredius, although it seems likely that Bode may have tried to acquire the picture for Berlin.

40 See Paul Tarnowski's essay "Dzików," available on www.tarnowski.com (accessed August 25, 2010).

41 For Frick's undated draft of his cable to Roger Fry, see Henry Clay Frick Art Collection Files, Series I: Purchases (Rembrandt Harmensz. van Rijn, *The Polish Rider*, Folder 1 of 4), TFC/FARL Archives.

42 Fry, as told to Osbert Sitwell; see Sitwell 1947, p. 350, note 135.

43 For the price, see *Paintings...* (see note 11), folio 99. Frick purchased *The Polish Rider* on April 20, 1910, for a total of $308,651.25, which included, besides the painting's cost ($293,162.50), a commission for Fry ($14,613.75), duty charges ($25), and the cost of a new frame ($850).

44 Frick to Fry, July 22, 1910, Henry Clay Frick Art Collection Files, Series I: Purchases (Rembrandt Harmensz. van Rijn, *The Polish Rider*, Folder 3 of 4), TFC/FARL Archives.

45 For their purchase price and date, and their return (on November 13, 1911), see ibid., folio 106, nos. 183–84 (as "Portrait of a Man in Broad-brimmed Hat and Ruff, 1633" [no. 183] and "Portrait of a Woman in White Cap and Ruff, 1634" [no. 184]).

46 "Frick and 'The Mill'—The Great Work Likely to Leave England," in *The Philadelphia Item*, March 9, 1911. A clipping is kept in Frick's Bill Book No. 2, p. 66, Henry Clay Frick Art Collection Files, TFC/FARL Archives.

47 For the offer of the "Saskia portrait," see Henry Clay Frick Papers, Series I: Art Files, Subseries V: Works Not Purchased (Rembrandt, Unnamed Work), TFC/FARL Archives. For the Nostitz picture, see Fry to Frick, May 16, 1911, Henry Clay Frick Papers, Series II: Correspondence (Fry, Roger E.), TFC/FARL Archives. For Olegar's offer, see Baron von Olegar, London, to Frick, June 20, 1911, Henry Clay Frick Papers, Series II: Correspondence (von Olegar, Baron), TFC/FARL Archives. For the Petersburg painting, see James de Vrescheville, Saint Petersburg, Russia, to Frick, June 21, 1911, Henry Clay Frick Papers, Series II: Correspondence (Vrescheville, James de), TFC/FARL Archives.

48 The "Saskia portrait," presently known as *A Young Woman as a Shepherdess* ("Saskia as Flora"), is now in the Metropolitan Museum, where it is attributed to Govert Flinck (1615–1660). Nostitz's "Rabbi," currently known as *A Scholar in His Study* (or *Biblical Figure at a Study Desk*) and still generally accepted as an autograph Rembrandt, is now in Prague's National Gallery. The other two (alleged) Rembrandts remain unidentified.

49 Fry to Frick, July 18, 1911, Henry Clay Frick Papers, Series II: Correspondence (Fry, Roger E.), TFC/FARL Archives.

50 Henry Clay Frick Papers, Series II: Correspondence (Fry, Roger E.), TFC/FARL Archives.

51 H. Silva White (on behalf of Feversham) to Frick, October 12, 1911, Henry Clay Frick Art Collection Files, Series II: Art Not Purchased (Rembrandt Harmensz. van Rijn, *The Dutch Merchant*), TFC/FARL Archives.

52 Fry to Frick, October 30, 1911, ibid.

53 Frick to Fry, November 13, 1911, ibid.

54 Frick to H. Silva White, November 14, 1911, ibid.

55 Frick to H. Silva White, April 27, 1912, ibid.

56 "Frick Buys a Rembrandt," in *The New York Times*, May 4, 1912, p. 1. Furthermore, days after Frick's death, the same paper reported that the Feversham painting was part of his collection; see "H. C. Frick's Paintings Which City Is To Have . . . ," December 7, 1919, ibid., p. XXI.

57 "$250,000 for Two Pictures; Bought by Americans, Who Continue to Drain Europe's Collections of Their Best," December 31, 1911, ibid., p. C1.

58 I wish to thank Morna O'Neill of Wake Forest University for bringing Lane's attempts to my attention. According to O'Neill, Lane's intermediary was probably John Quinn, the New York lawyer and collector of modern art. The Frick Archives hold no documentation regarding any interaction between Frick and Quinn.

59 Hugh Lane to Lady Augusta Gregory, August 8, 1912, in Lady Gregory Collection of Papers, Berg Collection of English and American Literature, New York Public Library.

60 Hugh Lane to Lady Augusta Gregory, February 13, 1914, ibid.

61 See Potterton 1986, cat. no. 808, pp. 124–27.

62 Lane dined with the Frick family on April 30, 1915, the day before the *Lusitania* sailed. The sale of his two paintings was handled entirely through two intermediaries, Alice Creelman and Henriette Lewis Hind. Creelman initiated the offer with Frick on April 2, 1915, and corresponded with him all along. Apparently, Lane was initially not aware that Frick was the buyer of his pictures, witness his letter to Frick of April 21, 1915, in Henry Clay Frick Papers, Series II: Correspondence (Lane, Hugh), TFC/FARL Archives. Frick authorized Bankers Trust Co. to remit £60,000 to Lane's estate on May 14, 1915; see Memorandum

voucher #4593, payable to Williams Deacon's Bank Limited for account of Estate of Sir Hugh Lane, May 17, 1915, Henry Clay Frick Papers, Series I: Art Files, Subseries I: Purchases, TFC/FARL Archives.

63 See sale cat. *Notable Paintings by Great Masters Belonging to the Estate of the Late M.C.D. Borden, Esq.*, American Art Association, New York, February 13–14, 1913, no. 28

64 Bredius visited Frick on November 1, 1913. His letter thanking Frick for his hospitality at Pride's Crossing is dated November 4, 1913; see Henry Clay Frick Papers, Series II: Correspondence (Bredius), TFC/FARL Archives.

65 Bredius, as cited in translation; see Buijsen 1990, p. 70.

66 Chas. C. Allom to Frick, May 7, 1914, One East 70th Street Papers, Series: Furnishings (White, Allom & Co.), TFC/FARL Archives.

67 "Famous Rembrandt Sold," in *The New York Times*, October 8, 1915, p. 3.

68 "Did Not Buy a Rembrandt. H. C. Frick Denies That He Purchased Portrait of Painter's Son," ibid., October 12, 1915, p. 11.

69 See, for example, Edward Brandus to Frick, March 10, 1915, Henry Clay Frick Papers, Series II: Correspondence (Brandus), TFC/FARL Archives; Wm. Rose, J. G. White & Company, New York, to Frick, October 30, 1916, Henry Clay Frick Papers, Series II: Correspondence (Rose), TFC/FARL Archives; Lewis & Simmons, Inc., New York, to Frick, February 24, 1917, Henry Clay Frick Papers, Series II: Correspondence (Lewis & Simmons), TFC/FARL Archives.

70 John Adams, diary entry for October 21, 1782, in Adams 1851, p. 295. Adams was appointed America's first Minister Plenipotentiary to Holland on April 19, 1782; he held this post until March 30, 1788.

71 For the price, see Memorandum voucher #5422, May 16, 1916, Henry Clay Frick Papers, Series I: Art Files, Subseries I: Purchases, TFC/FARL Archives.

72 Edward Brandus to Frick, May 12, 1916, Henry Clay Frick Art Collection Files, TFC/FARL Archives.

73 Bredius to Frick, October 19, 1916, Henry Clay Frick Art Collection Files, TFC/FARL Archives.

74 Frick to Carstairs, December 4, 1914, Henry Clay Frick Papers, Series I: Art Files, Subseries I: Purchases (Goya, *The Forge*, etc.), TFC/FARL Archives.

75 See chapter III, below. For the prices, see Invoice from M. Knoedler & Co., October 11, 1913, Bill Book No. 2,

p. 78, Henry Clay Frick Art Collection Files,
TFC/FARL Archives. *Farmyard with Tree and Figures*,
now doubted by some, cost £1,300 (or $6,321.25);
Landscape with Cottage, Trees, and Stream, still accepted,
and *Isaac Blessing Jacob*, now generally doubted, each
cost £600 (or $2,917.50).

76 Inventories of 1 East 70th Street made in the months
following Frick's death can be found in: Henry Clay
Frick Papers, Series: Estate Files, TFC/FARL Archives.

77 For the prices, see M. Knoedler & Co. statement of
account, May 31, 1916, Henry Clay Frick Papers, Series
I: Art Files, Subseries I: Purchases, TFC/FARL
Archives.

78 Knoedler invoiced Frick for the three etchings on
November 3, 1919, but did not submit the invoice to
HCF's estate for payment until February 13, 1920.
Papers pertaining to the purchase of these etchings,
including the invoice from M. Knoedler & Co., can be
found in Henry Clay Frick Papers, Series I: Art Files,
Subseries I: Purchases, TFC/FARL Archives.

79 See "H. C. Frick's Paintings Which City Is To Have…"
(see note 56).

II. *Catalogue of Paintings in The Frick Collection*

I. Rembrandt van Rijn
Portrait of Nicolaes Ruts, 1631

Oil on mahogany panel

46 x 34 ⅜ inches (116 x 87 cm)

The Frick Collection, New York (1943. 1.150)

Monogrammed and dated upper right: *R[H?]L. 1631*, and dated in the piece of paper: *1631*

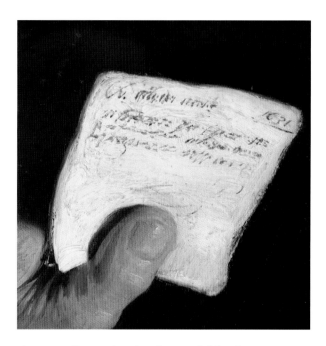

Fig. 1. Detail rotated to show letter in left hand

The Mennonite merchant Nicolaes Ruts (1573–1638) emerges confidently from a neutral background draped in a beautiful sable-lined gown known as a *tabbaard*, an antiquated garment associated with learning and tradition.[1] Around his neck is a set ruff or collar, and on his head, a fur hat. His large right hand rests on a leather chair, while his left holds a piece of paper with illegible writing, perhaps related to his business interests, and the date, 1631 (fig. 1).

Nicolaes Ruts was born in Cologne to a family of Protestant exiles from the Catholic city of Antwerp.[2] He was named after his grandfather Nicolaes Rutgeerts, nicknamed "Pels," the Dutch word for fur.[3] His father, David Rudtgeerts, was a silk trader who moved from Antwerp to Cologne in 1558 to escape religious persecution.[4] Nicolaes was married twice, first in 1594 to Cornelia Ranson and then in 1608 to Anna van Aperlo, and had a total of twenty-one children, fourteen of whom lived to adulthood. The family resided in the religiously tolerant city of Cologne until after 1612, when the new Archbishop Ferdinand of Bavaria expelled all Protestants. Nicolaes is mentioned in Mülheim by 1613 and recorded in Amsterdam in 1617, by which time he had become a member of the Reformed Church and shortened his name to Ruts.[5]

Little is known of Ruts's exact business in Cologne,

although documents indicate that he had built several houses in Mülheim. Later documents connect him to the large Dutch-dominated trade with Russia.[6] In the late sixteenth century the Dutch had built a colony in Arkhangel'sk in order to facilitate the buying of furs, including marten, ermine, wildcat, mink, wolf, arctic fox, squirrel, and, the most precious, sable, seen on Nicolaes's *tabbaard* in this portrait. In return, the Russians purchased needles, sabers, church bells, saffron, whale fins, woolens, silk, and velvet.[7] Nicolaes's son David is recorded as having offices in

Arkhangel'sk, perhaps working as an agent for his father.[8] At least initially, they do not seem to have prospered in Amsterdam. Apparently Nicolaes Ruts never owned his own house, but rented, moving at least twice to different houses on the Warmoesstraat in Amsterdam. In 1638—three months before he died—he filed for bankruptcy, a surprising result for a man who had been depicted so impressively by Rembrandt only seven years before.[9]

This strikingly handsome painting is generally considered to be Rembrandt's earliest commissioned portrait, completed soon after his move to Amsterdam from his native Leiden in 1631.[10] Before coming to Amsterdam, Rembrandt had executed history paintings in the style of his teacher, Pieter Lastman, as well as a number of self-portraits and sketches of heads known as *tronies*. The commission most likely came about as a result of Rembrandt's contact with the successful art dealer Hendrick Uylenburgh, to whom the artist had shrewdly loaned 1,000 guilders a few months before. This transaction could explain Rembrandt's move from Leiden to Amsterdam; it at least made that move possible. While Rembrandt did not aspire to be a portrait painter (he preferred the more important genre of history painting), portraiture was good business—those who bought portraits often went on to commission other paintings.[11] Rembrandt made more than forty portraits in the years 1631–35, no doubt to help him establish his career. Like Ruts, many of the sitters in Rembrandt's early portraits were Mennonite businessmen he met through Uylenburgh.[12] The close relationship between Rembrandt and the dealer resulted in the artist's marriage to Uylenburgh's cousin Saskia in 1634.

With his portrait of Nicolaes Ruts, Rembrandt announced his superior artistic abilities to the burghers of Amsterdam. With painstakingly fine and smooth brushstrokes, the artist created an extremely even surface on the panel, especially in the areas of the fabric and fur. For Ruts's multicolored whiskers, Rembrandt changed tactics and apparently used the butt-end of his brush to produce scratch marks that indicate the texture of the hairs. For the powerfully modeled face, he carefully juxtaposed multiple layers of varying colors. This technique created a liveliness and warmth in the portrait that herald Rembrandt's

emergence as one of the rare artists able to convey a deep psychological understanding of his subjects. Far from flattering Ruts, Rembrandt included heavy circles under his eyes that give him an intriguing air of concern and perhaps fatigue. The artist countered this impression by gently transitioning the background from a dark to a light gray and by turning Ruts at a subtle angle, thus creating a refreshing sense of movement in the composition. Such movement is largely absent in portraits by Rembrandt's Amsterdam contemporaries; Ruts's dynamic stance in fact is reminiscent of those pioneered a decade earlier by Van Dyck.[13]

An unusual feature of the painting is the support: it is one of the largest panels Rembrandt ever used and one of the few made from mahogany.[14] Mahogany was an uncommon wood in seventeenth-century Europe, having just been discovered in the West Indies at the end of the sixteenth century, and it is unclear how Rembrandt obtained it. Quite possibly it came from the sitter, whose activity as an international merchant would have given him access to rare and unusual materials. Many goods from around the world passed regularly through the ports of Amsterdam throughout the seventeenth century, a period when that city was a flourishing center of global trade.[15] The panel has unfortunately split in several places in the upper right, a not unusual occurrence for mahogany.

The painting has an uncommonly complete provenance, traceable to the family of the sitter. It remains, however, an open question whether Ruts or his daughter commissioned the portrait from Rembrandt. As mentioned, Nicolaes does not seem to have been the most successful businessman, renting the houses he lived in and filing for bankruptcy in 1638. His daughter Susanna and her husband Johannes Boddens, on the other hand, ran a thriving business as merchants in Amsterdam.[16] What is known definitively is that the painting was in Susanna's possession by 1636, when an inventory was made of her estate on the occasion of her second marriage to Pieter van der Hagen.[17] It descended through the family of Susanna's daughter Catherine Romswinckel and was copied in 1738 by either Frans van Mieris the Younger or Willem van Mieris.[18] At that time, it hung in Amsterdam, in the house of Abraham Romswinckel.

In 1799 an artist by the name of Abraham Delfos copied it for the drawing collection of Diederik, Baron of Leiden, in the home of Joost Romswinckel.[19] Happily, Delfos inscribed his drawing with the name of the sitter, whose identity would otherwise have been lost to posterity (fig. 3).[20] Indeed, by 1843 the picture was listed in an auction catalogue as "Portrait d'un Rabin" ("Portrait of a Rabbi").[21] Ruts's name was finally reattached to the portrait in 1883 when the great Rembrandt scholar Wilhelm Bode made the connection between the painting and the Delfos drawing, which itself had appeared in an Amsterdam sale in 1877.[22]

On January 12, 1807, a disaster occurred in Leiden that could have destroyed the portrait. Directly outside the door of Joost Romswinckel's elegant townhouse on the Rapenburg, a wooden ship with a cargo of 369 barrels of black powder exploded at 4:15 in the afternoon. All the houses in the immediate vicinity were either partially or completely destroyed, at least 151 people were killed, including one person in the Romswinckel household, and more than 2,000 were wounded, making this the deadliest explosion ever to have occurred in the Netherlands.[23] Miraculously, the Ruts portrait survived the explosion along with Romswinckel's collection of over 22,000 books, which he subsequently sold to King Louis Napoleon Bonaparte.[24]

In 1823 the Ruts was offered for sale as part of the collection of Anthony Meynts. While it is generally assumed that Meynts had bought the picture from the Romswinckel family sometime between 1817, when it was still with Joost Romswinckel,[25] and 1823, a previously little-known letter discusses the picture being offered to the Rijksmuseum in 1831 by the "Romswinckel Heirs."[26] In addition, in 1843 the picture is listed in a catalogue of Willem II's collection as having been acquired directly from the Romswinckel family.[27] A possible explanation for this discrepancy could be that the dealer Albert Brondgeest, who is listed as one of the organizers of the 1823 Meynts sale as well as the buyer of the Ruts portrait, had placed it

Fig. 3. Abraham Delfos (1731–1820), copy of Rembrandt van Rijn, *Nicolaes Ruts*, 1799, watercolor over black chalk, 20 x 15 ⅞ inches (50.7 x 40.2 cm), Rijksprentenkabinet, Amsterdam, inv. no. 1918.362

in the sale as a favor for the Romswinckel family, and it failed to sell at that time.

The fact that the picture was offered to the Rijksmuseum in 1831 by the Romswinckel heirs is not very well known. According to the letter mentioned above written by Cornelis Apostool, he felt it necessary to turn the picture down because of concerns of spending too much money during a financially and politically troubled time.[28] Rembrandt's portrait was subsequently bought by Willem I for his wife, Wilhelmina, of Prussia, who left it to her son Willem II, an avid art collector.[29]

In 1850 Willem II's large collection was sold at auction to pay an enormous debt to his brother-in-law, Nicholas I of Russia.[30] This sale was widely considered "one of the greatest blows ever dealt to Holland's

Fig. 4. View of Room 28, wall A, in the 1898 Rembrandt exhibition held at the Stedelijk Museum, Amsterdam, showing the Frick's portrait of *Nicolaes Ruts* and *Portrait of a Young Artist*

artistic heritage."[31] Along with the Ruts, the sale included seven other works attributed to Rembrandt, among them three now in The Wallace Collection, London: the *Portrait of Titus* and the pendants *Jean Pellicorne* and *Susanna van Collen;* and one now in The Metropolitan Museum of Art in New York: *The Noble Slav.*[32]

The painting eventually passed out of Holland into Adrian Hope's and then Joseph Ruston's collections and was shown in the famous Rembrandt exhibition of 1898 in Amsterdam, on loan from the collection of Comte Boni de Castellane of Paris (fig. 4). It hung near the Frick's *Portrait of a Young Artist* (cat. 4), and not too far from *The Polish Rider* (cat. 2) and *The Old Woman with a Book* (cat. 5). In 1899 *Nicolaes Ruts* was bought by the American financier J. Pierpont Morgan, whose son inherited it at his father's death in 1913. After Morgan Jr.'s death in 1943, the painting was purchased from his estate by the trustees of The Frick Collection, where it forms a perfect complement to the two other Rembrandts from the original Henry Clay Frick bequest.

L. W. R.

Provenance
Commissioned from the artist in 1631 by either Nicolaes Ruts, the sitter, or his daughter Susanna; in Susanna Ruts's possession by 1636; her second husband, Pieter van der Hagen (d. 1668); Susanna Ruts's daughter, Catherine Boddens Romswinckel (d. 1824), Lisse. By descent to Abraham Romswinckel, Amsterdam, by 1738. By descent to Joost Romswinckel, Leiden, by 1799 until after 1817. Sale, Amsterdam, Anthony Meynts collection, July 15, 1823, no. 107 (no title) (4,010 florins, to Albert Brondgeest, dealer, Amsterdam). Wilhelmina, Queen of the Netherlands (d. 1837); her son, Willem II of the Netherlands; his sale, August 12, 1850, no. 86 (as "Portrait d'un rabbin") (3,400 florins, to Weimar, dealer, The Hague); possibly from Weimar to Nieuwenhuys.★ Adrian Hope by 1883; sale, London, Adrian Hope collection, June 30, 1894, no. 57 (4,700 guineas, to Agnew). Joseph Ruston, Monk's Manor, Lincoln; sale, London, Joseph Ruston collection, May 21/23, 1898, no. 95 (5,000 guineas, to Colnaghi). E. Fischof, dealer, Paris; Comte Boni de Castellane, Paris. Charles J. Wertheimer, dealer, London, by 1899; sold by him for £6,000 to J. Pierpont Morgan, London and New York (d. 1913); his son, J. Pierpont Morgan, Jr., London and New York (d. 1943); purchased for $85,000 through M. Knoedler and Co., New York, by The Frick Collection in fall 1943.

★ Hinterding and Horsch 1989, p. 84.

Exhibitions
Stedelijk Museum, Amsterdam, *Rembrandt-Tentoonstelling,* 1898, no. 18bis, lent by Comte Boni de

34

Castellane; Royal Academy, London, *Old Masters Exhibition*, 1903, no. 43, lent by J. Pierpont Morgan; The Metropolitan Museum of Art, New York, *The Hudson-Fulton Celebration*, 1909, no. 77, lent by J. Pierpont Morgan; The Metropolitan Museum of Art, New York, *Loan Exhibition of the J. Pierpont Morgan Collection*, 1912–14, lent by J. Pierpont Morgan; Detroit Institute of Arts, *The Thirteenth Loan Exhibition of Old Masters, Paintings by Rembrandt*, 1930, no. 7, lent by J. Pierpont Morgan, Jr.; Knoedler Gallery, New York, *Paintings from the J. P. Morgan Collection*, 1943, no.16, lent by the Estate of J. Pierpont Morgan, Jr.

References
Amsterdam, Gemeentearchief, Records of the Notary Laurens Lamberti, NA 569, p. 64, March, 6, 1636. Scheltema 1817, vol. 2, p. 95; Nieuwenhuys 1843, p. 161, no. 75 (as "Portrait d'un rabin"). Vosmaer 1877, pp. 490, 495. Bode 1883, pp. 382–83, 587, 633, no. 215. Dutuit 1885, pp. 45, 62, no. 226. Bredius 1891, p. 74. Michel 1894, vol. 2, p. 236. Bredius 1899, p. 167. Moes 1905, pp. 297–98, no. 6627. Bode and Hofstede de Groot 1897–1905, vol. 1, pp. 134–35, no. 51, illustrated. Hofstede de Groot 1906, pp. 49–50, no. 49. Ward and Roberts 1907, vol. 2, n.p., illustrated. Valentiner 1908, p. 66, illustrated. Hofstede de Groot 1916, pp. 319–20, no. 670. Meldrum 1922/23, pp. 50, note 2, 187, pl. 64. Van Bemmelen 1929, pp. 59–69, fig. 2. Valentiner 1931, no. 12, illustrated. Bauch 1933, p. 217. Benesch 1935, p. 11; Bredius 1935, p. 7, no. 145, pl. 145. Martin 1936, p. 65, pl. 10. Van Gelder 1940, p.11. Scheurleer 1956, p. 28. Bauch 1966, pp. 18, 37, 41, pl. 348. New York 1968, pp. 252–57, illustrated. Fuchs 1968, p. 11, fig. 3. Gerson 1968, p. 206, no. 53, illustrated. Gerson 1969, pp. 128, 559, no. 145, illustrated. Haak 1969, pp. 70–71, figs. 104, 104a. Lecaldano 1969, p. 97, no. 66, illustrated. Slive 1970–74, pp. 113–14, fig. 110. Van Eeghen 1977, pp. 97–101. Strauss and van der Meulen 1979, pp. 136–37 (1636/4), illustrated. Schwartz 1984, pp. 146–47, no. 128, illustrated. Tümpel 1986, pp. 105, 411, no. 190, illustrated. Corpus 1986, vol. 2, pp. 115–21 (A43), fig. 1. Hinterding and Horsch 1989, pp. 5–6, 84, 86, fig. 1. Vels Heijn 1989, pp. 24–25, no. 9, illustrated. Slatkes 1992, pp. 242–43, no. 150, illustrated. Wright 2000, pp. 184–86, fig. 165. Chong 2001, p. 74, fig. 68. De Winkel 2006, pp. 26–30, fig. 1. Lammertse 2006, pp. 127–29, fig. 70. Schama 1999, pp. 333–37, illustrated. Straten 2005, pp. 220–21, fig. 296. Van Heel 2006, pp. 234–35, no. 199. Schwartz 2006, pp. 198–99, fig. 335.

NOTES

1 De Winkel 2006, p. 27.
2 Van Eeghen 1977, p. 97.
3 According to information provided by Max Rutgers van Rozenberg, a descendant of Nicolaes's brother, in an email to the author dated August 13, 2010, quoting information from the Archives Family Rutgers van Rozenburg, the Netherlands.
4 Perhaps David Rudtgeerts switched from his father's profession of trading in fur to trading in silk when the family moved to Cologne, a city without a seaport. This suggestion was made by Esmée Quodbach.
5 Elias 1903–5, vol. 2, pp.1001–2. Van Eeghen 1977, pp. 97–98, states that he was still in Cologne in 1613 and in Amsterdam by 1617. Van Bemmelen 1929, p. 65, found mention of him as having built houses in Mülheim in the summer of 1613. His brother's family retained the name Rutgers. Bemmelen lists Ruts's children on pp. 67–69.
6 Van Bemmelen 1929, p. 65; Van Eeghen 1977, p. 98, referring to notarial acts discovered by Simon Hart.
7 Schama 1999, pp. 335–36.
8 Van Bemmelen 1929, pp. 65–67; Scheltema 1817, vol. 1, pp. 116–17.
9 Van Eeghen 1977, p. 98.
10 The *Seated Scholar* in St. Petersburg is also dated 1631; it is not known which was painted first.
11 See Corpus 1986, pp. 91–98, for a list of how these commissions evolved.
12 On Rembrandt's contact with Uylenburgh, see Lammertse 2006.
13 Slive 1970–74, p. 114, rightly pointed out how the placement of Ruts's hands is similar to that in several portraits by Frans Hals, including Hals's *Portrait of a Man* in The Frick Collection (1910.1.69). However, while Hals's man fills the space entirely, Ruts appears to emerge actively from the background, thus introducing a fascinating narrative element that is lacking in the Hals. Ruts's *tabbaard* was originally wider, and the letter extended to the left. These seemingly small changes lend the picture much of the dynamism it displays. See Corpus 1986, p. 117.
14 Corpus 1986, p. 119.
15 Apparently some of Rembrandt's later, smaller mahogany panels were previously used as boxes to import sugar from Central America. See Van de Wetering 2009, p. 16.
16 Van Eeghen 1977, p. 99. Dudok van Heel 2006, pp. 234–35, note 199, feels fairly strongly that the commission was from Susanna, since there is no pendant portrait of Nicolaes's second wife, and normally portraits would be passed down to sons, not daughters.

Fig. 2. Unknown artist, copy of Rembrandt van Rijn, *Nicolaes Ruts*, inscribed *Rembrandt f. 1638*, oil on panel, 31 ½ x 25 ½ inches (80 x 65 cm), Sale, Heberle, Cologne, December 9–10, 1892, lot 156

17 Her first husband had died. See Hofstede de Groot 1906, pp. 49–50, no. 49. A record of the inventory is contained in *The Montias Database of 17th-Century Dutch Art Inventories* available through The Frick Collection Web site.

18 Drawing in the Backer Foundation, Amsterdam, Willet-Holthuysen Museum. (See van Bemmelen 1929, p. 61, fig. 3.)

19 Van Eeghen 1977, p. 97. A previously unpublished high-quality oil-on-wood copy of the Ruts was sold at auction in Cologne in 1892 (fig. 2). It is unknown when or by whom the copy was produced.

20 The inscription pasted down on the mount reads: "Het portrait van Nicolaas Ruts Levensgroote geschildert door Rembrant van Rijn 1632 [*sic*]. Naar het Origineel getekend door Abm Delfos 1799. thans berustende bij den Heer Joost Romswinkel te Leyden." ["The life-sized portrait of Nicolaas Ruts painted by Rembran[d]t van Rijn 1632 [*sic*]. Drawn after the original by Ab[raha]m Delfos 1799 currently owned by Mr. Joost Romswinkel of Leyden"]. The letter is inscribed: "Rembrandt Pinx./A. Delfos del./1799." Another inscription in pencil on the back lower left-hand corner reads: "het Portrait van Nicolaas Ruts na een Schilderij van Rembrand Levens groote verbeeld . . . getekend door A. Delfos 1799."

21 Nieuwenhuys 1843, p. 161, no. 75.

22 Bode 1883, pp. 382–83. The drawing was given to the Rijksprentenkabinet in 1918 by the purchaser at the 1877 sale, Dr. C. W. J. J. Pape, The Hague.

23 For a complete description of the 1807 explosion, see Reitsma and Ponsen 2001, pp. 507–14.

24 Korteweg 2006, p. 7. Bonaparte eventually placed the books in the Koninklijke Bibliotheek, The Hague.

25 Scheltema 1817, vol. 2, p. 95.

26 Director of the Rijksmuseum, Cornelis Apostool, to "Adm OK & W" (Administratie Onderwijs, Kunsten en Wetenschappen [Commissioner of the Ministry of Education, Arts and Sciences]) dated February 25, 1831, Rijksmuseum archives, Haarlem, with the subject: "Advies op de Rekweste van de Erven van J. Romswinckel" (Advice on the petition of the heirs of J. Romswinckel).

27 Nieuwenhuys 1843, p. 161, no. 75.

28 The letter was brought to light by Scheurleer 1956, p. 28.

29 The identification of the "Queen of the Netherlands" mentioned in earlier provenances must refer to Wilhelmina. In Willem II's 1843 collection catalogue (see note 21), the painting is listed as having been given to him by "La feue Reine" (the late queen). Wilhelmina had died in 1837, whereas Willem II's wife was Anna Pavlovna.

30 See Hinterding and Horsch 1989, pp. 4–122.

31 Hofstede de Groot, "Kunstverzamelingen van ons vorstenhuis," in *Stemmen des Tijds*, vol. 12 (1923), p. 158, mentioned in Hinterding and Horsch 1989, p. 8, note 6, where other complaints are also discussed.

32 Hinterding and Horsch 1989, p.8 and cat. nos. 84–91. The other three are no longer attributed to Rembrandt, and there have been doubts about the Pellicorne couple. The Frick's *Deposition* by Gerard David (1915.1.33) was also in the sale, where it was attributed to Jan Gossart. See ibid., cat. no. 35.

2. Rembrandt van Rijn
The Polish Rider, c. 1655

Oil on canvas

46 x 53 ⅛ inches (116.8 x 134.9 cm)

The Frick Collection (1910.1.98)

Inscribed on rock at the extreme right: *R[e?]*

Rembrandt's painting of a youthful long-haired rider in Polish dress, armed with two swords, a war hammer, a bow, and a quiver of arrows—three of which are placed carefully in the front leather pocket of the quiver—remains one of his most haunting and mysterious works. The serene, open expression of the rider contrasts with the barren, unforgiving nocturnal terrain through which he and the horse proceed at some speed. In the more thinly painted background, we discern a domed citadel with fortified buildings atop a hill, and, at right, a ridge of trees leading down to the tower that overlooks a pool or stream at whose edge a fire is burning faintly.[1]

The young man's red fur-lined cap, or *kuczma*, and his long riding coat, known as a *joupane*, were of the kind customarily worn by Polish (and Hungarian) light cavalry officers during the seventeenth century. Yet for all their specificity, they are accouterments whose significance is hard to assess.[2] *The Polish Rider* has less to do with equestrian portraiture than with genre painting—the exotic horseman had long been a favored subject of printmakers[3]—yet the large scale of the canvas and the dignity of the protagonists, both man and beast, elevate the subject to the realm of myth or allegory.

Try as they may, historians have been unable to find any narrative—biblical, historical, or literary—that satisfactorily explains the subject of Rembrandt's

painting.[4] And while the presence of a number of well-born Polish students enrolled at the universities of Leiden and Franeker in the 1640s and 1650s seemed to offer a possible solution to the enigma—all the more tantalizing in light of the work's late eighteenth-century Polish provenance—attempts to assign a specific sitter or particular commission to *The Polish Rider* have failed as well.[5] In an unsurpassed analysis, refined over several years, Julius Held stressed the symbolic, generalizing qualities of this unusual work. Rather than approaching the painting through the lens of portraiture, Held interpreted the composition as "a glorification of youthful courage and dedication to a worthy end," identifying the young warrior as a latter-day crusader or Christian knight: a "Miles Christianus."[6]

The canvas has undergone several alterations. As is confirmed by X-radiography (fig. 1), a strip of approximately ten centimeters was added to the lower edge of the composition to replace the original canvas that had presumably deteriorated beyond repair. This addition may date to the end of the nineteenth century, and in early photographs of *The Polish Rider* the two hoofs in this section appear more solidly planted on the ground, in a straight line, with cast shadows indicated horizontally to the right (fig. 2).[7] In his restoration of *The Polish Rider* in 1950, Frick conservator William Suhr reconstructed the nineteenth-century addition, repainting the hoofs and removing the cast shadows.[8] As a consequence, the horse has appeared to some viewers to be less

Fig. 1. *The Polish Rider*, X-radiograph, Sherman Fairchild Center for Paintings Conservation, The Metropolitan Museum of Art

anchored to the terrain.[9] It is possible that the picture may have been trimmed on the right-hand side at some point early in its history, since most of the signature has been removed, and the boulder at lower right is truncated.[10]

Rembrandt's handling and touch in *The Polish Rider* also merit discussion, as does the painting's condition. Certain well-preserved sections are described in meticulous detail and finish: the horse's head, neck, harness, and bit; the rider's face, jacket, and weapons. Other areas—notably the sky and buildings in the background, the terrain, the horse's legs and hindquarters—are much more sketchy in appearance. For the English artist Walter Sickert, writing in 1910, the "whole landscape" was "full of Courbet."[11] Van de Wetering has remarked upon these discrepancies in technique and raised the question of whether certain

parts of the composition may have been unfinished, or brought to completion rapidly by Rembrandt (or another artist) in order to include the work in one of the bankruptcy sales that were organized in 1656–57. Citing Houbraken's reminiscence that Rembrandt was "so quick to change and move on to other things that many of his works were only half-way finished," van de Wetering has tentatively proposed that some areas—the horse's legs and hindquarters, the landscape and terrain in the background—may have remained in a more or less preliminary stage, with the grayish-brown ground partly exposed.[12]

Known only to a handful of specialists until its discovery in a remote Galician estate in 1897 by Abraham Bredius (1855–1946), the director of the Mauritshuis who was traveling on an extended trip to Russia and Poland, *The Polish Rider* was the "chief

Fig. 2. Archival photograph of *The Polish Rider* taken in 1950, before restoration

sensation" of the Rembrandt exhibition that opened in September 1898 at the recently built Stedelijk Museum in Amsterdam.[13] In that exhibition, the picture was catalogued as "a Polish rider in the uniform of the Lysowsky regiment," a reference to the Polish condottiere Alexander Lisowski (d. 1616), whose regiment of mercenaries had disbanded in the 1630s.[14] Although no documents exist with regard to the seventeenth-century ownership of *The Polish Rider*, an important discovery in the Czartoryski archives in Cracow established the earliest provenance of the painting.[15] It is first mentioned in August 1791 in a letter from Michael Casimir Ogiński (1728–1800), grand hetman of Lithuania, to Stanisłaus Augustus Poniatowski (1732–1798), the art-loving king of Poland who was rapidly assembling a collection of

Old Master paintings that now form the core holdings of Dulwich Picture Gallery in London.[16]

> I am sending Your Majesty a Cossack, whom Reinbrand [*sic*] had set on his horse. This horse has eaten during his stay with me for 420 German gulden. Your Majesty's justice and generosity allow me to expect that orange trees will flower in the same proportion.[17]

It would appear that Ogiński was bartering the Rembrandt, possibly acquired recently on the Dutch or German art market, for items from the royal orangery at the Lazienzki Palace suitable for the estate he was laying out at Helenow Castle, near Warsaw. In a royal inventory of 1793, the picture is again described as representing "un Cosaque à Cheval." It is noteworthy that these late eighteenth-century references made no mention of the work as a family portrait, nor did they identify the rider as Polish.[18]

Until quite recently, scholarship on *The Polish Rider* had revolved around the identity of the youthful rider and the narrative associated with his nocturnal journey. The sources for Rembrandt's composition were first laid out by Julius Held, who catalogued the costume and weaponry, established the prints and book illustrations to which Rembrandt may have turned in his elaboration of the subject, and cited, as a model for the somewhat cadaverous horse, the contemporary anatomical theaters in Leiden and Amsterdam that the artist was known to frequent.[19] The focus of enquiry shifted radically in 1984, when Josua Bruyn—a founding member of the Stichting Foundation Rembrandt Research Project— tentatively reattributed *The Polish Rider* as an early work by Rembrandt's student Willem Drost (1633–1659).[20] The ensuing controversy, which breeched the academic and curatorial arenas to become something of a cause célèbre in the 1990s, has been calmed, if not definitively settled, by Ernst van de Wetering's magisterial study, which concluded that *The Polish Rider* was laid out by Rembrandt and painted substantially by him, with another artist possibly from his studio completing the work in order to make it more presentable for sale.[21]

Following Held and van de Wetering, and building upon Marieke de Winkel's research into Rembrandt's use of costume, we should return to the topicality of subjects with a Polish resonance for Dutch painters and patrons in the 1650s. Certainly, Rembrandt's delight in exotic paraphernalia and arms and armor, which he collected, extended to Polish costume and military accouterments.[22] The pomegranate-shaped

Fig. 3. Ferdinand Bol (1616–1680), *Portrait of Otto van der Waeyen in a Polish Costume*, 1656, oil on canvas, 62 ¼ x 47 ½ inches (158 x 120.5 cm), Museum Boijmans Van Beuningen, Rotterdam

boss with leather strips that holds the swinging tassel of horsehair and is attached to the horse's leather bridle in *The Polish Rider* will reappear as the sash ornament at lower right in Rembrandt's *Self-Portrait* in 1658 (see cat. 3). Polish hats, shoes, and boots were inventoried among the possessions of several artists of Rembrandt's generation for use as studio props.[23] The association of Poles with military valor was an established trope, which also extended to fashionable portraiture. Ferdinand Bol's portrait of eight-year-old Otto van der Waeyen, son of an Amsterdam civil servant, signed and dated 1656 (fig. 3), shows the boy in a yellow *joupane* with small buttons, scarlet breeches, yellow-brown boots, and a fur cap, all of which appear in Rembrandt's *Polish Rider*, as does the war hammer that the boy holds in his right hand.[24] The Polish-Lithuanian Commonwealth was a source of grain, timber, and fur for Dutch merchants and an important trading partner. Sympathies for the Polish cause may have been heightened in the second half of the 1650s, when the Poles and Russians were involved in the Second Northern War against Sweden. If the image of the valiant Polish nobleman had a special piquancy at this time, might Rembrandt have intended his youthful rider with his many martial attributes to satisfy a topical and patriotic appeal among collectors of contemporary Dutch painting?

C.B.B.

Provenance

Purchased in 1791 by Michael Casimir Ogiński, grand hetman of Lithuania (1728–1800); purchased from him in 1793 by Stanisław II Augustus Poniatowski, king of Poland (1732–1798), Warsaw; inherited in 1798 by his nephew Prince Józef Antoni Poniatowski (1763–1813); inherited in 1813 by Countess Marie-Thérèse Tyszkiewicz (1765–1834); purchased from her June 13, 1814, by Prince Franciszek Ksawery Drucki-Lubecki (1778–1846); purchased from him by 1815 by Count Hieronim Stroynowski, bishop of Vilnius, (1752–1815); inherited by Senator Valérien Stroynowski (1755–1834), Volhynia; inherited in 1834 by Countess Valérie Stroynowska (1782–1849) and included in her dowry upon her marriage to Jan Feliks Tarnowski (1777–1842), Castle Dzików, Galicia; inherited by their direct heir, Jan Dzierżysław Tarnowski (1835–1894); inherited by Count Zdzisław Tarnowski (1862–1937), Castle Dzików, Galicia; purchased in 1910 by Henry Clay Frick through Roger Fry for $307,776 (including Fry's commission).

Exhibitions

Stedelijk Museum, Amsterdam, *Rembrandt-Tentoonstelling*, 1898, no. 94, lent by Count Tarnowski; Carfax Gallery, London, June 1910; Museum of Fine Arts, Boston, *Loan Exhibition of Pictures from the Collection of Henry C. Frick*, December 1–15, 1910, no. 2, lent by Henry Clay Frick.

References

Bode 1883, p. 499. Michel 1893, pp. 373, 560. Michel 1894, vol. 2, p. 232. Bredius 1897, pp. 197–99. Amsterdam 1898, no. 94. Hofstede de Groot 1898, no. 94, illustrated. Nicolle 1898, p. 558. Bredius 1899, p. 194. no. 94. Bell 1899, p.135. Bode and Hofstede de Groot 1897–1905, vol. 6 (1901), p. 163–64, no. 466, illustrated. Wurzbach 1906, p. 573. Valentiner. 1908, p. 563, illustrated p. 435. Wurzbach 1910, p. 399. Lotus 1910, pp. 7–8. Holman 1910, p. 887. Boston 1910a, p. 1, no. 2. Boston 1910c, p. 46. Wurzbach 1911, p. 91. Hall 1911, p. 504. Roberts 1912, p. 147, illustrated p. 148. Hofstede de Groot 1916, p. 163, no. 268. American Art News 1916, p. 1. Art World 1917, p. 377, illustrated p. 376. Valentiner. 1921, illustrated p. 435, no. 466. Meldrum 1922/23, plate 355. Friedländer 1926, illustrated p. 210. Valentiner 1930, pp. 3–4, pl. XVIII. Valentiner 1931, no. 121, illustrated. Hind 1932, pp. 90–91, pl. LXVI. Bredius 1936, p. 12, no. 279. Siple 1936, p. 102. Woolf 1940, pp. 150–51. Held 1944, pp. 246–65. Sickert 1947, pp. 161–164, 350. Hamann 1948, pp. 392, 396–97, illustrated, p. 457. Martin 1948, no. 71, illustrated. Rosenberg 1948, vol. 1, pp. 150–52, 228; illustrated in vol. 2, fig. 217. Valentiner 1948, pp. 129–35. Pittsburgh 1949, pp. 126–27, no. 58. Bühler. 1949, p. 93, illustrated pl. 32. Hanfstaengl 1949, p. 125, 130, illustrated pp. 126–27. Rotterdam 1956, pp. 163–64. Gerson 1956, p. 280. Lorentz 1956, pp. 13, 15, 18. Yourcenar 1957, pp. 127–28. Ciechanowiecki 1960, pp. 294–96, illustrated fig. 1. Goldscheider 1960, p. 178, no. 87, illustrated. Rosenberg 1964, pp. 251–56, illustrated p. 254. Żygulski 1965, pp. 43–67. Bauch 1966, p. 12, no. 211, illustrated. Clark 1966, pp. 36–40, illustrated p. 37. Gimpel. 1966, pp. 95–96. New York 1968, pp. 258–65, illustrated. Fuchs 1968, pp. 49–50, illustrated no. 90. Massar 1968, illustrated p. 176. Białostocki 1969, illustrated p. 163. Gerson 1969, p. 571, no. 279. Held 1969, pp. 45–84, illustrated. Munhall and Grier 1970, pp. 6, 74–75, illustrated. Campbell 1970, pp. 292–303, illustrated fig. A. Kannegieter 1970, pp. 85–88. Haverkamp-Begemann 1971, pp. 95, 98–99. Roberts 1972, p. 406. Sutton 1972, p. 330. Campbell 1973, pp. 126–36, illustrated pl. 21, fig. 86. Broos 1974, illustrated p. 192. Danto 1974, p. 140. De Coo 1975, p. 116, illustrated p. 115. Haussherr 1976, pp. 55–56. Bailey 1978, pp. 130–31. Bolten and Bolten-Rempt 1978, no. 434, pp. 144–45, illustrated p. 139. Clark 1978, pp. 59–60. Deyell 1980. Chrościcki 1981, illustrated p. 442. Lowenthal 1981, pp. 13–14. Kitson 1982, no. 34, illustrated. Slatkes 1983, pp. 59–91, illustrated, 133–44. Baudiquey 1984, p. 208, illustrated p. 216. Białostocki 1984, pp. 16, 18. Bruyn 1984, p. 158. Hoving 1984, p. 45. Quick 1985, p. 551. Schwartz 1985, pp. 273, 277–78, illustrated, 330. Koning 1986, p. 106, illustrated. Hochfield 1987, p. 109. Alpers 1988, pp. 59, 124, illustrated pl. 4.35. Brown 1989, p. 8. Slatkes 1989, p. 140. Watson 1989, p. 341. Bailey 1990. Bal 1991, pp. 349–55, illustrated p. 350. Broos 1991a, pp. 16–18, illustrated. Broos 1991b, pp. 52–56. Held 1991, pp. 194–99, illustrated. Liedtke 1992, p. 143, illustrated. Bal and Bryson 1992, p. 530. Brown 1992, p. 272. Slatkes 1992, pp. 68–70, no. 28, illustrated p. 69. Van Thiel 1992, pp. 44–45. Wardle 1992, p. 126. Broos 1993, p. 289. Tümpel 1993, no. 123, illustrated p. 304. Bailey 1994. Janas and Wójcik 1994, pp. 27, 107–11, illustrated p. 167. Stansky 1996, pp. 80–81. New York 1996, p. 6.

Sanger 1998, pp. 72–75 (illustrated), 315, 350, 452–54 (illustrated). Schatborn 1998, p. 71. Binstock 1999, pp. 154–56, illustrated. Cómez Ramos 1999, pp. 135–42. Schama 1999, p. 603, illustrated. Solkin 1999, pp. 224–26, illustrated. Zygas 1999, pp. 6–10, 31. Dilworth 2000: 215–25, p. 224. Haskell 2000, p. 103. Wright 2000, pp. 162–64, illustrated fig. 147. Żygulski 2000, pp. 197–205. Bedaux and Ekkart 2000, pp. 237–39. Van de Wetering 2001, pp. 22–24, illustrated. Bikker 2002, p. 147, no. 1. Bailey 2002, pp. 10–12, illustrated. Scallen 2004, pp. 130, 132, 149, 201, 349 note 6, illustrated p. 128. Bikker 2005, pp. 147–49, no. R16, illustrated p. 148. Crenshaw 2006, p. 142, illustrated p. 145. Schwartz 2006, p. 369. Gregorovich 2007, pp. 5–10. Saltzman 2008, pp. 161, 219–23, illustrated with color plates, n.p. Brunet 2009, p. 101. Quodbach 2009, pp. 1, 8. Van de Wetering 2009, pp. 207, 209, 210–11, illustrated p. 209. Corpus 2010, pp. 535–50, no. V 20, illustrated p. 536.

NOTES

1   This entry is indebted to Ernst van de Wetering and Marieke de Winkel's entry on *The Polish Rider*, recently published in Corpus 2010, pp. 535–50, a draft of which was submitted to The Frick Collection in August 1997. Some of the authors' conclusions were published in Van de Wetering 2001, pp. 22–24, and Van de Wetering 2009, pp. 207–11. See also the thorough and judicious entry on the picture in New York 1968, pp. 258–65.

2   Held 1944, pp. 253–55; Held 1969, pp. 59–64; Żygulski 1965, pp. 43–67.

3   Abraham de Bruyn's costume plates of Hungarian and Polish military figures date from the late sixteenth century; Stefano della Bella's circular etchings of foreign cavalry appeared around 1651 and were most likely known to Rembrandt; see Held 1944, p. 265; Held 1969, pp. 257–58.

4   Among the subjects that have been proposed are the departure of the prodigal son (Campbell 1970, pp. 292–303); the young King David setting out to fulfill Saul's conditions for the betrothal to his daughter Micah (Slatkes 1983, pp. 85–90); Tamerlane pursuing Bayazet outside Constantinople, a scene from the play *Tamerlane* by Joannes Serwouters, first performed in Amsterdam on September 5, 1657 (Schwartz 1985, pp. 277–78).

5   For an interpretation of *The Polish Rider* as an equestrian portrait of a member of the Ogiński dynasty, see Broos 1974, and Chrościcki 1981. For the problems posed by these identifications, see Held 1991, pp. 197–98.

6   Held 1969, pp. 83–84.

7   New York 1968, pp. 258–65. The entry notes that the picture may have been restored in Vienna in 1877, and that it was treated by Hauser in Berlin in preparation for the Amsterdam exhibition of 1898.

8   Suhr's fully documented "Record of Treatment" can be consulted in the records of The Frick Collection's Conservation Department.

9   Corpus 2010, p. 538, notes that the horse's legs have become "slightly longer than the artist intended," and that this might account for "the impression of instability caused by horse and rider."

10   Unlike the repair of the lower strip, the reduction in width would have taken place before 1795; in that year an inventory of the Lazienzki Palace in Warsaw gave the dimensions as 109 x 133.9 cm, the width of the canvas today; see Held 1944, p. 248, and New York 1968, p. 260.

11   Sickert 1947, p. 163; he reviewed the picture for *The New Age* on June 23, 1910, while it was on view at the Carfax Gallery in London.

12   Van de Wetering 2009, pp. 210–11. The author has noted the stylistic similarities between *The Polish Rider* and Rembrandt's *Moses Breaking the Tablets of the Law*, signed and dated 1659 (Gemäldegalerie, Berlin), which he also considers to be an unfinished picture.

13   Haskell 2000, pp. 102–3. Scallen 2004, pp. 129–32, quotes Bredius's impassioned reaction on first seeing the picture in the collection of Count Tarnowski, published in an article in *De Nederlandsche Spectator* in 1897: "One glance at the whole, an examination of several seconds of the technique was all that was necessary for me to be instantly convinced that here in this remote place one of Rembrandt's greatest masterpieces had hung for almost one hundred years."

14   Hofstede de Groot 1898, no. 94, "Portret van een Poolsch Ruiter in de uniform van het regiment van Lysowsky." Ciechanowiecki showed that this romantic identification was made by an early nineteenth-century owner of the painting, Countess Valerie Tarnowska, whose distant forebear, Colonel Stroynowski, had commanded the Lisowski regiment during the Thirty Years' War (Ciechanowiecki 1960, p. 296).

15   Ciechanowiecki 1960, pp. 294–96.

16   On Poniatowski's collecting, see, most recently, Salomon 2010, pp. 15–17.

17   Ciechanowiecki 1960, p. 295.

18   Held 1944, p. 247; Ciechanowiecki 1960, p. 295.

19 Held 1944, especially pp. 260–63.

20 Bruyn in his review of the first volumes of Werner
    Sumowski's *Gemälde der Rembrandt-Schüler* (Bruyn 1984,
    p. 158). Early in the twentieth century Alfred von
    Wurzbach had catalogued *The Polish Rider* as by Aert
    de Gelder, an attribution that gained no adherents.
    The debates unleashed by Bruyn's reattribution are
    summarized in Bailey 1994. The reattribution to
    Drost is rejected in Bikker 2005, pp. 147–49, who also
    provides an excellent summary of the debates around
    the painting's subject and authorship.

21 Corpus 2010, pp. 543–44. See also Van de Wetering
    2001, pp. 22–24, and Van de Wetering 2009,
    pp. 203–211.

22 De Winkel 2006, pp. 215–16.

23 Ibid, pp.160, 346, 348, 350.

24 Bedaux and Ekkart 2000, pp. 237–39.

3.

Rembrandt van Rijn
Self-Portrait, 1658

Oil on canvas

52 ⅝ x 40 ⅞ inches (133.7 x 103.8 cm)

The Frick Collection (1906.1.97)

Signed and dated on the arm of the chair at right: *Rembran../ f. 1658*

In the largest of Rembrandt's painted self-portraits, executed when he was fifty-two years of age, the artist assumes a frontal pose, hieratic in conception.[1] He places himself "embarrassingly close in the foreground of the picture plane," so much so that his silver-topped cane at lower right almost teeters into the viewer's space.[2] Light enters from the upper left, casting deep shadows over the sitter's left cheek, shoulder, and arm, and rendering the folds of his velvet and fur cape even more mysterious. But this light also illuminates the sitter's upper body, made corpulent by the layers of costume, and casts its brightest spot on the right hand and sleeve above, untroubled by shadow. Although Rembrandt portrays himself seated—one is tempted to say, enthroned— we see only the curved molding of the wooden chair's left arm peeking out below the sitter's left hand, whose fingers seem barely able to grasp the cane.

Two pieces of canvas, from the same bolt, were required for the portrait; the vertical seam is visible through the sitter's left shoulder. Examining the canvas weave and patterns of cusping along all four edges, Ernst van de Wetering concluded that the canvas may have been as much as nine centimeters higher at the top, and wider by five centimeters on both the left and right sides.[3] However, new X-radiography, made by Dorothy Mahon during her recent cleaning of the *Self-Portrait* (fig. 1), confirms rather that the canvas in its present state retains its original dimensions.[4]

The X-radiograph also demonstrates that Rembrandt painted this magisterial composition directly, with extraordinary sureness of touch but that he came to the distinctive frontal pose only after considerable revision. Initially, Rembrandt seems to have placed himself in a more conventional three-quarter pose, with his proper left shoulder and arm receding diagonally into the background and his upper body angled appropriately. Different attributes—possibly a sword, a shield, or a scabbard—may have been shown resting against his stomach and thigh, finally to be replaced by the vertical rattan cane and somewhat flaccid fingers of his left hand. As Rembrandt readjusted his pose to assume the definitive full-square presentation, he also changed the position of the sash and raised the upper part of it accordingly.[5] The change most visible to the naked eye was in the placement of the weighted end of the sash, initially painted closer to the sitter's crotch. The shape of Rembrandt's beret may have also been somewhat modified: its current, scalloped form differs from the obliquely rising contour documented in the X-radiograph.[6]

Rembrandt's technique in the Frick *Self-Portrait* is a consummate example of his late manner, aptly described a century ago as "a rough, rugged aggregation of seemingly formless touches."[7] Richly impastoed throughout, the paint is applied thickly, in layers, with broken surfaces and highlights that emphasize the tactility of the picture plane. In his life

Fig. 1. *Self-Portrait*, X-radiograph, Sherman Fairchild Center for Paintings Conservation, The Metropolitan Museum of Art

of the artist, Arnold Houbraken spoke of portraits by Rembrandt in which the paint had been applied so thickly that one could lift the painting from the ground by its nose.[8] Such effects of facture, thoroughly mediated, became part of Rembrandt's signature style in the last decade of his life. Examination of some of the most virtuosic passages in the *Self-Portrait*—particularly the face and hands, the brocaded neck cloth, the upper section of the jerkin—reveal the pains that Rembrandt took in the construction of his rough manner, applying pink glazes to thickly painted flesh tones, and glazing the freely painted highlights of the knuckles and thumb with reddish hues. The sonorous colors of the costume are given additional warmth and vibrancy by the dramatic handling of light and shade.[9]

For all its theatricality, Rembrandt's self-portrait was an honest description of a man who looked older than his fifty-two years. Comparison with the artist's last etched self-portrait (fig. 2), dated the same year and showing him seated at a table with his etching needle, confirms the particulars of his appearance at this time.[10] In the print, Rembrandt's hands, while large, appear more refined and nimble than in the Frick *Self-Portrait*. Van de Wetering remarked on the rarity of Rembrandt's depicting both hands so prominently in any of his painted self-portraits and speculated that he might have used a model in this instance.[11] Certainly, it is hard to imagine that the hand holding the cane would have been capable of the dexterity required to work on the tiny etching plate.

It has long been recognized that the Frick's monumental *Self-Portrait* was executed during a period of constraint and adversity, when Rembrandt was facing financial, professional, and, it can be assumed, personal difficulties. After declaring bankruptcy in July 1656, for the next two and a half years he and his family warded off debtors and sold his vast collections in a series of public auctions.[12] In February 1658 Rembrandt vacated and sold the house and studio on Sint Anthonisbreestraat he had occupied since May 1639, moving to rented accommodation on the Rozengracht in the Jordaan, "a neighborhood of bell foundries, sailors' taprooms, and saltpeter works."[13] A poignant indication of this diminished existence is the accident that took place outside the Lommert, the city's pawnshop, in May 1658, when a "large mirror in a black frame" that Rembrandt's son, Titus, had bought back from one of the sales of his father's goods was broken by the workman charged with transporting it.[14] Such mirrors would have been used in the production of large-format three-quarter-length self-portraits.

How far such well-documented biographical information helps illuminate the significance and meaning of the Frick *Self-Portrait* has been much debated in recent scholarship. It is anachronistic to look for expressions of personal or private concerns in Rembrandt's painted self-portraits, made for art

Fig. 2. Rembrandt, *Self-Portrait, Etching*, 1658, etching, 4 ¹¹⁄₁₆ x 2 ½ inches (11.8 x 6.4 cm), Graphische Sammlung Albertina, Vienna (DG1930/562)

lovers who wished to own examples of his work in an immediately recognizable style.[15] While we do not know the earliest owner of the Frick *Self-Portrait*— and are generally ill-informed about how Rembrandt marketed his late work to collectors in Amsterdam (and beyond)—it is the case that Rembrandt and his contemporaries would not have considered the genre of self-portraiture a vehicle for self-examination or the exploration of identity.[16] A more fruitful line of inquiry treats the self-portraits as a type of "self-representation" and attends to seventeenth-century modes of commemoration.[17] Approached as a historiated self-portrait, in which Rembrandt makes reference to his celebrated Northern predecessors, the Frick *Self-Portrait* does indeed address issues of status and tradition, with the aging artist—shown neither at work nor in studio attire—asserting his claim to be considered a lineal descendant of Apelles, the Prince of Painters.[18]

Shrouded in a voluminous cape or cloak, a patchwork of furs, Rembrandt is shown with his black beret placed above a reddish-brown headband; his golden-yellow pleated jerkin, or paltrock, with its low horizontal neckline, is worn over a linen shirt, fastened diagonally. An ornamental neck cloth of gold brocade is tucked into the front of the jerkin, and a red sash is wound twice around the waist; from its end hangs a silver pomegranate. In his left hand the sitter holds a silver-tipped jointed cane, probably of rattan, imported from East Asia; it is similar to the one that will appear in Rembrandt's portrait of the wealthy merchant Jacob Trip (The National Gallery, London), painted three years later.[19] This accouterment has been occasionally misidentified as a maulstick, although there are no brushes or palette in sight.[20]

As he often did in both his painted and etched self-portraits, in the Frick *Self-Portrait* Rembrandt portrayed himself in early sixteenth-century costume, with the fanciful addition of certain elements of exotic or Eastern dress.[21] His customary beret or "bonnet"—in this instance with scalloped edges[22]—had been worn by "all classes in various forms and usually of black colour" in the first decades of the sixteenth century, but had long dropped out of fashion.[23] Because of Rembrandt's inclusion of it in his self-portraits, the beret had become an attribute of the artist, even though it was not part of the painter's working attire. The yellow jerkin was also an item of historical costume from the same period. Rembrandt may well have been familiar with Karel van Mander's reference to such an article of clothing in his Life of Lucas van Leyden. In describing a meeting between Lucas and the Flemish painter Jan Gossart, van Mander had praised the "very stately manner" of the latter, "resplendent in a garment of gold cloth." Not to be outdone, Lucas was dressed "in a jerkin of yellow silk camlet which in the sunshine also had the luster of gold."[24] An avid collector of prints, Rembrandt would also have been familiar with engraved portraits of Lucas and Gossart (fig. 3) in his illustrated compendium *Pictorum aliquot celebrium Germaniae inferioris effigies*

(*Portraits of Some Celebrated Artists of the Low Countries*), first published in 1572 and expanded by Hendrik Hondius in 1610.[25]

If such engraved portraits provided Rembrandt with accurate models for historical costume and headwear, Jacobus Neeffs's print after Van Dyck's portrait of the one-armed landscape painter Maarten Ryckaert, published in the Iconographia of 1630–45, has been identified as a possible source for the distinctive frontal pose of the Frick's *Self-Portrait* (fig. 4). Marieke de Winkel was also the first to note that the white linen garment fastening diagonally across the chest worn by Rembrandt under his yellow paltrock was an example of Eastern or Polish clothing, similar to a kaftan. Along with the sash and its pomegranate pommel, these were exotic elements, redolent of luxury.[26]

By such means does Rembrandt attach himself to a distinctly Northern pantheon of artists, claiming a place in the historical canon of Netherlandish art, a successor to the most famous Northern Renaissance master who shared his birthplace in Leiden and was celebrated as both a painter and an engraver. From this perspective, Rembrandt's indebtedness in the Frick *Self-Portrait* to Titian and sixteenth-century Venetian models is to be found primarily in his rugged handling of paint and liberated brushwork.[27]

There remains the poignancy of Rembrandt's fashioning of identity at a time of such personal and professional adversity, which recent scholarship, skeptical of an overdetermined biographical approach, has tended to dismiss. Confronting the Frick *Self-Portrait* soon after its arrival in New York in the first decades of the twentieth century, observers were moved by the pathos of the artist's "self-representation" (hardly a term that would have been available to them). In his review for *The Burlington Magazine* of the Hudson-Fulton exhibition at The Metropolitan Museum of Art in 1909, the American painter and critic Kenyon Cox (1856–1919) wrote with feeling of Frick's "romantic Rembrandt . . . larger than life, colossal in its size as in its rugged handling. . . . It is the head of an old lion at bay, worn and melancholy, yet conscious of its strength, determined and a little defiant."[28] For the dealer René Gimpel (1881–1945), who was received by Frick in his West Gallery in March 1919, the *Self-Portrait* was the collector's finest

Fig. 3. *Portrait of Jan Gossart* from Dominicus Lampsonius's *Pictorum aliquot celebrium Germaniae inferioris effigies,* published by Hieronymus Cock, 1572, engraving, Rijksprentenkabinet, Amsterdam

Fig. 4. Jacobus Neeffs after Anthony Van Dyck, Portrait of Maarten Ryckaert from the Iconographia, 1630–45, engraving, 9 ½ x 6 ⅛ inches (24.2 x 15.7 cm), Rijkspresentenkabinet, Amsterdam

picture: "Huge hands grip the chair. A wise and human potentate, whose eyes fix on the beholder and overwhelm him."[29]

Thus, it is somewhat surprising to discover that the earliest recorded reaction to Rembrandt's *Self-Portrait* was unexpectedly critical. It was made a century earlier, in May 1815, when the painting was placed on public exhibition for the first time, lent by the third Earl of Ilchester to the British Institution's summer exhibition of *Pictures by Rubens, Rembrandt, VanDyke and Other Artists of the Flemish and Dutch Schools.*[30] In the barely legible annotations to a copy of the exhibition catalogue in a compendium held at the Frick Art Reference Library, a well-informed and opinionated commentator—an artist or dealer, no doubt—described Rembrandt's *Portrait of Himself* in distinctly unflattering terms. "He is holding a stick

and looks like a great butcher. Unpleasing: fine as to colour and composition."[31]

C.B.B.

Provenance

[Possibly Stephen Fox-Strangways (baptized Stephen Fox), first Earl of Ilchester (1704–1776), Redlynch House, Somerset, and, c. 1758 on, Melbury House, Dorset; inherited by Henry Thomas Fox-Strangways, second Earl of Ilchester (1747–1802), Melbury House, Dorset, 1776]; possibly inherited in 1802, but certainly in the possession, by 1815, of his son Henry Stephen Fox-Strangways, third Earl of Ilchester (1787–1858), Melbury House, Dorset; inherited by his half-brother William Thomas Horner Fox-

Strangways, fourth Earl of Ilchester (1795–1865), Melbury House, Dorset, 1858; inherited by his nephew Henry Edward Fox-Strangways, fifth Earl of Ilchester (1847–1905), Melbury House, Dorset, 1865; inherited by his son Giles Stephen Holland Fox-Strangways, sixth Earl of Ilchester (1874–1959), Dorset and London(?), 1905; purchased jointly by Otto Gutekunst of Colnaghi's and Charles Carstairs of Knoedler and Co., November 1906, kept at Colnaghi's London; purchased by Henry Clay Frick for $225,000 in December 1906 (payment made January 1907).

Exhibitions
British Institution, London, *Pictures by Rubens, Rembrandt, VanDyke, and Other Artists of the Flemish and Dutch Schools,* May 1815, no. 30, lent by Henry Stephen Fox-Strangways, third Earl of Ilchester; Royal Academy, London, *Exhibition of Works by Old Masters and by Deceased Masters of the British School: Winter Exhibition,* January–March, 1889, no. 157, lent by Henry Edward Fox-Strangways, fifth Earl of Ilchester; Royal Academy, London, *Works by Rembrandt: Winter Exhibition,* January 2–March 11, 1899, no. 61, lent by Henry Edward Fox-Strangways, fifth Earl of Ilchester; The Metropolitan Museum of Art, New York, summer 1907, lent by Henry Clay Frick; Union League Club, New York, *An Exhibition of Paintings from the Collection of Mr. Henry C. Frick,* January 9–12, 1908, no. 10, lent by Henry Clay Frick; The Metropolitan Museum of Art, New York, *Hudson-Fulton Celebration,* 1909, no. 102, lent by Henry Clay Frick; Museum of Fine Arts, Boston, *Loan Exhibition of Pictures from the Collection of Henry C. Frick,* December 1–15, 1910, no. 1, lent by Henry Clay Frick.

References
London 1815, p. 15, no. 30. Smith 1836, p. 90, no. 225. London 1883, p. 7, no. 16. London 1889, no. 157. Michel 1894, vol. II, pp. 115–16, 236, frontispiece. London 1899, no. 61. Bell 1899, p. 82. Bode and Hofstede de Groot 1897–1905, vol. 6 (1901), p. 90, no. 428. Moes 1905, vol. 2, p. 315, no. 58. Burroughs 1907, vol. 2, p. 126, no. 7. New York 1908a, no. 10. New York 1908b, p. 20, no. 29. American Art News 1908, vol. 6, no. 13 p. 1, illustrated. Holmes 1908, vol. 13, no. 65, pp. 306–9, illustrated pl. 1. Valentiner 1908, p. 562, illustrated p. 400. Bode 1909, illustrated facing p. 8. Valentiner 1909, p. 103, no. 102. American Art News 1909, vol. 7, no. 35, p. 2. Cox 1909, vol. 16, no. 81, pp. 183–84. Waldmann 1910, p. 75, note 1. Wurzbach 1910, p. 403. Holman 1910, p. 887. Boston 1910a, no. 1. Boston 1910c, p. 46. Boston 1910b. American Art News 1910, vol. 9, no. 8, p. 2.

Holmes 1911, pp. 167–69. Roberts 1912, vol. 34, p. 147, no. 135. Collins-Baker, n.d., no. 2, illustrated. Hofstede de Groot 1916, vol. 6, p. 277, no. 563. Meldrum 1922/23, p. 199, no. 337, illustrated. Van Dyke 1923, pp. 37–38. Hind 1932, pp. 19, 149, frontispiece. Valentiner 1930, vol. 28, p. 4, no. 30. Valentiner 1931, pl. 133. Bredius 1935, p. 4, no. 50. Siple 1936, p. 102, no. 395. Van Gelder 1948, p. 50, illustrated p. 47. Hamann 1948, p. 122–23, illustrated fig. 88. Rosenberg 1948, vol. 1, pp. 30, 171, 199, illustrated vol. 2, fig. 40. Pittsburgh 1949, vol. 1, pp. 128–29, no. 59. Pinder 1950, pp. 94–96, illustrated p. 93. Müller Hofstede 1963, , pp. 65–68, no. 2, illustrated. Clark 1966, p. 130, illustrated p. 129. Bauch 1966, p. 17, no. 329, illustrated. Gimpel 1966, pp. 95–96. Erpel 1967, pp. 45–46, 183–84, no. 93. New York 1968, pp. 266–68, illustrated. Gerson 1969, p. 551, no. 50. Rheims 1969, pp. 42–47. Munhall and Grier 1970, pp. 6, 76–77. Beneschol 1973, vol. 5, pp. 314–15, no. 1176. Clark 1978, p. 28, illustrated p. 29. De Vries 1978, p. 89, fig. 56, p. 109, note 2. Wright 1982, p. 32, no. 7, illustrated pl. 87. White 1984, p. 138, illustrated p. 131. Bonafoux 1985, pp. 110–13, illustrated. Schwartz, 1985, pp. 350–51, illustrated. Sutton 1985, pp. 139–40, illustrated p. 154. Alpers 1988, p. 86, illustrated p. 64, fig. 3.71. Slatkes 1989, pp. 139–44. Le Bot 1990, pp. 14, 26, illustrated p. 116. Chapman 1990, pp. 88–97, 121, illustrated pl. IV. Pächt 1991, pp. 11, 77, illustrated p. 43. Bal 1991, pp. 251–55, illustrated p. 252. Slatkes 1992, no. 272, illustrated p. 411, no. 273. New York 1996, p. 65. Sanger 1998, pp. 57, 306, 488, illustrated p. 64. Schama 1999. pp. 616–17, 638, illustrated p. 618. White and Buvelot 1999, p. 198, no. 71, illustrated, pp. 11–12, and p. 70, illustrated. Berger 2000, pp. 479–95, illustrated pl. 29. Haskell 2000, p. 161. Westermann 2000, pp. 4, 315, illustrated p. 6. Wright 2000, pp. 329–30, illustrated p. 333. Rosand 2000, p. 13, illustrated. Scallen 2004, pp. 197, 201, illustrated p. 200. Quodbach 2004–5, p. 104. Corpus 2005, pp. 460–68, no. IV.14, illustrated, and pp. 74–76. Crenshaw 2006, pp. 153–55, illustrated. Schwartz 2006, p. 211, illustrated p. 210. De Winkel 2006, pp. 183–87, illustrated p. 184. Liedtke 2007, vol. 2, p. 688, illustrated p. 690, fig. 191. Chapman 2008, pp. 38, 44, illustrated p. 39. Saltzman 2008, pp. 180–96, 213, illustrated. Quodbach 2009, p. 236. Van de Wetering 2009, pp. 221, 290, illustrated pp. 217, 219.

NOTES

1 This entry is indebted above all to the excellent discussions in Chapman 1990, pp. 88–97, and Corpus 2005, pp. 460–68.

2 Corpus 2005, p. 465.

3 Ibid, p. 462.

4 I am grateful to Dorothy Mahon, who, in creating new X-radiographs of the *Self-Portrait,* has noted the outlines of the original strainer on the left-hand edge and upper and lower edges of the canvas. The absence of a strainer impression on the right-hand edge suggests that the support was cut from a larger piece of primed canvas that originally extended to the right.

5 In examining the structure of the body color in the

right-hand section of the X-radiography, Mahon noted that the initial placement of the figure of the seated artist was far from the distinctive hieratic pose of the finished work. Her technical examination has been invaluable in the preparation of this entry.

6   Corpus 2005, p. 464.

7   Holmes 1908, p. 309.

8   From Houbraken's three-volume *De groote schouburgh der Nederlantsche konstschilders en schilderessen* (1718–21, cited by Ernst van de Wetering in White and Buvelot 1999.

9   Van de Wetering (in Corpus 2005, p. 465) has noted a development in Rembrandt's style from the mid-1640s, "to find alternatives to the spotlight effect and the sacrifice of colour. His solution seems to be larger areas of colour stemming from a more frontal lighting of frontally placed forms and figures."

10 White and Buvelot 1999, p. 199. Kenneth Clark (1978, p. 30) noted that he appears "well filled out and solid looking" in this "completely straightforward record of his appearance."

11 Ernst van de Wetering in White and Buvelot 1999, p. 12.

12 Crenshaw 2006.

13 Schama 1999, p. 620.

14 Berlin, Amsterdam, and London 1991–92, p. 61.

15 Ernst van de Wetering (in White and Buvelot 1999, pp. 28–31) has approached Rembrandt's production of self-portraits as part of an enterprise to manufacture and disseminate fame; for collectors, the painted self-portraits would have been prized as "specimens of Rembrandt's exceptional technique."

16 Gary Schwartz's intuition that such a monumental work as the Frick *Self-Portrait* would have fitted comfortably in a gallery formed by one of the crown heads of Europe, while impossible to substantiate, is well founded: "I cannot imagine this, the largest and most overwhelming of the self-portraits, hanging anywhere but in the collection of someone whose own portraits were commensurately larger and whose dignity could bear comparison." Schwartz 1985, p. 350. Ruminating on this insight, van de Wetering (2005, p. 468) noted the presence of a large self-portrait by Rembrandt in the collection of the Amsterdam merchant Sibert van der Schelling, described in March 1711 as "an incomparable portrait, very large, of Rembrandt painted by himself."

17 Corpus 2005, p. 462.

18 Chapman 1990, p. 92.

19 For the *Portrait of Jacob Trip*, c. 1661, see Schwartz 2006, p. 211, and Bomford, et al. 2006, pp. 166–71.

20 Chapman 1990, p. 121, where the "staff" in the Frick *Self-Portrait* is interpreted as "alluding to both a king's scepter and the painter's mahlstick."

21 Ibid., pp. 91–92; and especially De Winkel in Corpus 2005, pp. 45–46, 60–64, 71–77, and De Winkel 2006, pp. 163–88. As de Winkel has noted (2005, p. 46), Rembrandt rarely appeared in his self-portraits in the same formal, fashionable clothes as his patrons.

22 Similar to the headwear in the *Self-Portrait* of 1652 in the Kunsthistorisches Museum, Vienna, in which, unlike in the Frick picture, Rembrandt is dressed in working clothes; see White and Buvelot 1999, pp. 190–91, and Corpus 2005, pp. 410–17.

23 De Winkel 2006, pp. 166–67.

24 Van Mander's anecdote is cited in Corpus 2005, p. 466; see also the discussion in De Winkel 2006, pp. 166–67, pp. 185–86.

25 De Winkel in White and Buvelot 1999, pp. 68–69; De Winkel 2006, pp. 166–67, pp. 183–87.

26 De Winkel in White and Buvelot 1999, pp. 70–71; Corpus 2005, p. 467.

27 See Clark 1966, pp. 123–30, and Chapman 1990, pp. 92–93, for a discussion of the relationship with Titian. The significance of the more local, Northern tradition is argued in Corpus 2005, p. 467, and, most recently, in the excellent essay in Chapman and Woodall 2010, pp. 10–17.

28 Cox 1909, pp. 183–84. Rembrandt's *Self-Portrait* was installed in a commanding position in one of the exhibition's Dutch rooms; see the installation shot reproduced in Haskell 2000, pp. 158–59.

29 Gimpel 1966, p. 96, "March 3, At Henry Frick's."

30 On the first public exhibition of Old Masters held in the United Kingdom, see Fullerton 1982, p. 68, and Haskell 2000, pp. 64–67. The Ilchester Rembrandt was displayed in the North Room, dominated by Van Dyck's *Charles I on Horseback* (The National Gallery, London).

31 See the "Catalogue of Pictures by Rubens, Rembrandt, Van Dyke and Other Artists of the Flemish and Dutch Schools," in London 1815, pp. 1–21, bound in *London, British Institution, Catalogues 1813–1852*, New York, The Frick Art Reference Library, E L84 B77.

4. Follower of Rembrandt van Rijn
Portrait of a Young Artist, 1650s

Oil on canvas

39 ⅛ x 35 inches (99.4 x 88.9 cm)

The Frick Collection, New York (1899.1.96)

Signature and date (neither part of the original paint layer) inscribed at upper right: *Rembrandt f: 164[?]*

This work by a follower of Rembrandt, most likely produced in Amsterdam in the 1650s, is as much a portrayal of painting as it is a portrait of an individual artist. The sitter, a fashionable young man with a mustache and mouche, dressed in a fine black cloak and an imposing hat, holds an album of large sheets of paper, the edges and corners of which catch the light. Between the thumb and forefinger of his proper right hand, he holds a paintbrush; just beyond its tip, a pile of brushes rests on the cloth-covered table at left.[1] The canvas or panel on which he paints, or pretends to paint, is absent. Instead the focus is divided between his warmly lit face and the album he holds. On the visible sheet or back cover of this album, a drawn or etched image appears—perhaps a sketch this artist made expressly for the unseen painting in progress or some pre-existing drawing or print he is consulting as a model; a figure's face and upraised arm can be made out at the top of the page (fig. 1). Although the sitter's pose identifies this work as a formal portrait, the picture may also be understood as part of a contemporary proliferation of images of painters at work, comprising portraits, self-portraits, studio scenes, and other genre depictions, in which Dutch artists pictured their craft and through which they promoted their profession.[2]

Inscribed at upper right with Rembrandt's name and a 1640s date (the last numeral is cut off), this painting was long thought to be by the master himself. After more than 150 years of publication with this unquestioned attribution, beginning with the painting's appearance in a 1766 Paris sale, the work's authorship was challenged for the first time in a controversial book of 1923 by the American art historian John C. Van Dyke.[3] Scholars promptly rejected Van Dyke's revision of Rembrandt's oeuvre by contesting his generally flawed method and ignoring his specific deattributions, thereby restoring this work and others to autograph status, though not without acknowledging that some revision to Rembrandt's oeuvre was in fact needed.[4] In the course of conservator William Suhr's technical examination and treatment of the Frick painting in 1948, he discerned inconsistencies with Rembrandt's technique and further determined that the signature and date at upper right were not part of the original paint film and thus probably added at some later date.[5] The simultaneous sea-change in Rembrandt connoisseurship, which witnessed such scholars as Jakob Rosenberg, Kurt Bauch, and Horst Gerson substantially reducing and reshaping the artist's oeuvre, brought with it the permanent deattribution of the Frick picture.[6] From 1948 onward the painting has been published as the work of a pupil or follower, a view upheld today on the basis of its facture and technique.

While a few specific artists have been named in discussions of the work's authorship—Barent Fabritius, a pupil of Rembrandt's in the 1640s, was the first and

Fig. 1. Detail of *Portrait of a Young Artist*

the most frequent proposal—the work cannot securely be placed in any individual painter's oeuvre.[7] Attempts to identify the artist portrayed have also yielded intriguing hypotheses but no conclusive results.[8] At this time, we can only place the work and, with it, its model and maker in Rembrandt's orbit some time in the 1650s, taking into account the portrait type (common in Amsterdam portraiture from the 1630s through the 1650s), the tall hat and gold embroidered shirt fashionable from the 1640s through the 1660s,[9] and the style, most likely derived from Rembrandt's work of the 1650s. The painting in fact exhibits some diversity of style, represented at one end by the controlled brushwork and traditional modeling of the black cloak and at the other by the strikingly summary rendering of the paintbrushes on the table at left. It is more likely that this painting dates from or after the years in which Rembrandt was consistently painting, even in formal portraits, in a broad manner, as in his portrait of Nicolaes

Bruyningh of 1652 (Staatliche Kunstsammlungen, Kassel) and Jan Six of 1654 (Six Collection, Amsterdam).

Even if the Frick picture remains far shy of the master's bold touch, the application of the paint points to a desire to approximate Rembrandt's technique by an artist who did not have a deep understanding of it, evidenced particularly by the rapid execution of the gold buttons that gleam but do not suggest shape or volume; the unblended paint in the face, which gives it a ruddy appearance instead of the illusion of subtle curves and depressions; the modeling of the hands, particularly the proper right, in the uppermost paint layer with peach-colored highlights that seem to hover over the surface rather than read as illuminated flesh. New X-radiographs of the Frick painting, taken and analyzed in August 2010 by Dorothy Mahon, paintings conservator at The Metropolitan Museum of Art, corroborate these observations, showing a more diffuse application of lead white to build up flesh tones. Other passages, however, suggest that this artist was an experienced and confident painter and most likely not a pupil. The rapidly painted yellow embellishment of the hat, which, although difficult to read—and hence variously described as ribbon, leaves, lace, "trail of blossom," and even corn—is a palpable representation of glinting light. The long, loose strokes of gray and white of the album, applied over an intermediary ocher layer applied on top of the red tablecloth and black cloak, end in feathery touches of the brush that effectively represent the soft corners of the individual sheets and evoke the materiality of the paper and the light that falls on it.

Dorothy Mahon's recent examination of the work has determined that William Suhr's removal in 1948 of the five-inch strip of canvas from a different painting that had been added to the top of the original canvas by the time the painting appeared in Paris in 1766 indeed restored the painting to close to its original dimensions.[10] The painter thus conceived this work as it appears today, with the figure filling the composition, top to bottom, left to right. His pose in combination with the setting and his accouterments serves to present the man as if in midaction, pausing in thought as he paints and, conveniently, looking up and outward at the viewer to satisfy the work's function as a portrait. This was a popular mode of presentation for portraits of scholars, ministers, and other subjects for whom writing and reading was a frequent activity. Rembrandt's portraits of an unidentified gentleman known as *A Scholar* of 1631 (State Hermitage Museum, St. Petersburg), his and Jacob Backer's portraits of the minister Johannes Wtenbogaert of the mid-1630s (Rijksmuseum, Amsterdam), and Rembrandt's etched portrait of the calligrapher Lieven van Coppenol of c. 1658, for example, present their subjects seated at tables covered with books and papers and either interrupted and distracted from their work or pausing in quiet contemplation. Rembrandt himself portrayed artists in a similar fashion, as in his etched portrait of the painter Jan Asselijn of 1647/48 and the *Self-Portrait with Saskia* of 1636.[11] That this last print figured into the final design of the Frick picture is suggested by the striking way in which the eyes are shaded by the brim of the hat in each image; in the case of the Frick painting, the artist in fact enlarged the hat as he painted, perhaps to achieve this very effect.[12] At the same time, in both prints by Rembrandt, the subjects appear in more static poses; the papers on the table before Jan Asselijn bear no clear relation to the canvas behind him (itself burnished out in the second state of the print), while in the self-portrait Rembrandt draws on the paper before him. In the Frick picture, the artist studies the image on paper in his hands. The work thus cleaves more closely (and deliberately so) to the portraits of scholars and similar representations of apostles and scholar-saints. In this vein, it bears relation to depictions of artists by the Leiden master and former Rembrandt pupil Gerrit Dou. The maker of the Frick picture did not follow directly or exclusively Rembrandt's examples but responded and contributed to a broader tradition of representations of artists in the Dutch Republic.

In his works dating from the 1630s through the 1660s, Dou often incorporated this mode of presentation into genre scenes representing artists, scholars, and conflations of the two.[13] In his *Self-Portrait* of c. 1665 in The Metropolitan Museum of Art (fig. 2), for example, the painter, identifiable as such by the brushes and palette he holds, reads a book—a textual

Fig. 2. Gerrit Dou (1613–1675), *Self-Portrait*, c. 1665, oil on panel, 19 ¼ x 15 ⅜ inches (48.9 x 39.1 cm), The Metropolitan Museum of Art, New York, Bequest of Benjamin Altman, 1913 (14.40.607)

visual source, holding in his hands both album and brush, linking head and hand, thought and execution.[14]

Rembrandt never portrayed an artist consulting a drawing or print as he paints, though he depicted artists drawing after sculpture and live models. Painting after drawn or printed images was, however, a standard studio practice, one directly linked with the concept of emulation as it was understood in the seventeenth century. It was primarily through prints and drawings that artists knew the works of antiquity and the more recent past, while original print compositions by Albrecht Dürer and Lucas van Leyden were also taken as prestigious models worthy of selective appropriation.[15] Such material, along with a painter's own sketches, studies, and designs, were kept in studios as a visual repertory from which to derive imagery and inspiration. Later in the century, artists like Adriaen van Ostade and Michiel van Musscher would commonly present painters working with such material at hand, sometimes pinned to the top of an easel or a nearby wall or scattered on the floor. Vermeer's *Art of Painting*, in fact, features a bound set of prints or drawings, very similar to that in the Frick painting, on the table beside the artist, most likely intended to be read as a source he consults as he paints his live model.[16] The creative appropriation of sources was in keeping with the early modern understanding of artistic originality, as it was discussed and debated in contemporary written theory.[17] This notion was also expressed in pictorial tributes to artists such as the engraved portrait of Frans Floris in Dominicus Lampsonius's *Pictorum aliquot celebrium Germaniae inferioris effigies* (Portraits of some celebrated artists of the Low Countries), first published in Antwerp by Hieronymus Cock in 1572 (fig. 3). In this print, the Flemish painter holds a brush, palette,

source perhaps for his painting in progress. In other works by Dou, painters engage in different forms of mental stimulation such as smoking or playing musical instruments, often with their easels in the distant background or, as here, omitted altogether. With these pictures, artists forged a visual resemblance and conceptual association between contemporary painters and thinkers of the past and the present, offering a statement on art-making as an intellectual and dignified pursuit. The Frick picture makes its own claim for painters and painting through its specific presentation of a painter contemplating a maulstick, and a two-dimensional depiction of a standing nude. The inclusion of the nude is intended as a nod to Floris's reputation as a painter of classical subjects, but the choice to present it on this hand-held white rectangle (possibly a drawing tablet, a foreshortened album like the one in the Frick painting, or a print or a drawing mounted on board) rather than in a painting on an easel is to emphasize Floris's study and creative emulation of his sources as the key to his success as a painter of antiquity.[18] The Frick painting also celebrates this part of the artistic process, showing the artist contemplating his source material as he paints and thereby emphasizing such intellectual activity as a fundamental part of painting.

Our sitter, however, is attired not like a scholar in a robe, or *tabbaard*, but in a stylish and expensive hat, a luxurious cloak of heavy and fine material, and a shimmering green-gold doublet with gleaming gold buttons.[19] Fashionable contemporary dress is of course standard in formal portraits and, through the early seventeenth century, in self-portraits and studio scenes as well.[20] Yet by midcentury, other options were available, and for an artist who was emulating Rembrandt and participating in the same artistic discourse as Dou, choosing fashionable rather than the work clothes and exotic, historical dress in which Rembrandt attired himself or the *tabbaard* or fancy dress of Dou's scholarly painters was not a given.

In such images of painters as fashionable gentlemen, artists acknowledged and advertised their membership in yet another class of society, that which earned its wealth, and in large sums. This identification with the merchant class is reflected in the painter Philips Angel's speech to the painters' guild of St. Luke in Leiden in 1641 and its subsequent publication under the title *In Praise of Painting*. In this celebration of the art of painting, Angel relates a story by the Dutch poet Jacob Cats about a beautiful maiden who must choose a husband from among suitors of different professions.[21] The irony of the verses extolling the mercenary painter's worthiness over that of the poet, who receives for his beautiful verse only laurel, myrtle, and praise, is suppressed in Angel's retelling.[22] He recasts this tale as genuine praise of painters as earners, noting that "Painting is of far greater profit and use than poetry for sustaining the body."[23] As scholars have shown, in the mercantile

Fig. 3. *Portrait of Frans Floris*, from Dominicus Lampsonius's *Pictorum aliquot celebrium Germaniae inferioris effigies*, published by Hieronymous Cock, 1572, engraving, 8 ⅞ x 5 ¼ inches (22.6 x 13.3 cm), Rijksprentenkabinet, Amsterdam

society of the Dutch Republic, earning a good living and "nobility," in the broad sense of the word, were not mutually exclusive and rather were, in the views of some and in the reality of many Dutch painters' lives, unavoidably aligned.[24] The Frick picture may be an independent expression of a similar idea through visual means. As a combination of a portrait of an artist in fashionable dress and a depiction of an artist at work—thinking and painting—this image hovers between categories of representation and both derives and departs from Rembrandt's example to present painters as members of both the intellectual and the economic elites.

The drawn or etched image on the album that is the most virtuoso passage in the painting (see fig. 1) is difficult to decipher, but the raised arm of the figure could suggest an image of victory, something like the frontispiece of the 1610 edition of Lampsonius's *Effigies* published in The Hague of Hendrik Hondius. There, putti hover in the air amid swirling drapery in an allegory of painting's emancipation as a liberal art.[25] By midcentury this was an old idea, but one complicated by the realities of the burgher society of the Dutch Republic and thus worth restating in new ways, both in written form and in paint.

J.S.

Provenance

Jacques-André-Joseph Aved (1702–1766), Paris; his sale November 24, 1766, no. 34, as a portrait of Lenard Bramer [*sic*]. (Annotations in the Frick Art Reference Library's copy of this 1766 sales catalogue note a sale price of 152 livres and, illegibly, a name, possibly the buyer.) George Howard, sixth Earl of Carlisle (1773–1848) by 1836, Castle Howard, Yorkshire; inherited in 1848 by his son George William Frederick Howard, seventh Earl of Carlisle (1802–1864), London (and Yorkshire?);* inherited in 1864 by his brother William George Howard, eighth Earl of Carlisle (1808–1889), Castle Howard, Yorkshire; inherited in 1889 by his nephew George James Howard, ninth Earl of Carlisle (1843–1911), Castle Howard, Yorkshire; jointly purchased in 1897 by Asher Wertheimer and J. and P. Colnaghi & Co, London; Arthur Tooth and Sons, New York; purchased in 1899 for $38,000 by Henry Clay Frick, Pittsburgh and, later, New York.**

* Waagen (1854, p. 280) lists the work as being in Carlisle's London town house. As Esmée Quodbach notes in her essay in this volume, Harriet Beecher Stowe wrote in 1853 that she had seen the painting there.

** A letter of June 8, 1988, from Martha Hepworth, Assistant Provenance Archivist, Getty, to Bernice Davidson, then Research Curator at the Frick, in the curatorial file, notes Colnaghi's and Wertheimer's purchase of the painting from Lord Carlisle in 1897, citing transactions documented in a microfiche copy of Colnaghi's stock records. As she points out in this letter, this identifies the lender of the painting to the 1898 Amsterdam exhibition, recorded in the catalogue as W** of London, as Wertheimer. See also Cynthia Saltzman 2008, pp. 145–46, 159–63, and Esmée Quodbach's essay in the present volume.

Exhibitions

The British Institution, London, June 1853, no. 21, as a portrait of Leonard Bramer, lent by the Earl of Carlisle; Stedelijk Museum, Amsterdam, *Rembrandt-Tentoonstelling*, 1898, no. 70, lent by Asher Wertheimer; The Metropolitan Museum of Art, New York, *Hudson-Fulton Celebration*, 1909, no. 92 as "Portrait of a Young Man," lent by Henry Clay Frick;

Museum of Fine Arts, Boston, 1910, no. 3, lent by Henry Clay Frick.

References

Paris 1766, no. 34 (as a portrait by Rembrandt of Lenard Bramer [*sic*]). Smith 1836, vol. VII, p. 122, no. 338 (as by Rembrandt). London 1853, no. 21 (as a portrait by Rembrandt of Bramer). Waagen 1854, p. 280 (as "a male portrait" by Rembrandt). *The Athenaeum* 1876, p. 469, column 3 (as a "Portrait of a Pupil" by Rembrandt). Bode 1883, p. 580, no. 149 (as a painting of a young artist by Rembrandt, c. 1648). Dutuit 1885, p. 42 (as by Rembrandt). Michel 1893/94, vol. 1, p. 235, p. 63 (a portrait by Rembrandt, c. 1648, possibly of the artist Jan van de Cappelle). Amsterdam 1898, no. 70 (as a portrait by Rembrandt of a young painter, c. 1648). Hofstede de Groot 1898, no. 70 (identically as in Amsterdam 1898). Bredius 1899, p. 193 (as a portrait by Rembrandt of the artist Jan van de Cappelle). Bell 1899, p. 140 (as by Rembrandt). Bode and Hofstede de Groot 1897–1905, vol. 5 (1901), p. 144, no. 365, illustrated (as by Rembrandt, c. 1648). Valentiner 1908, p. 560, illustrated p. 345 (as by Rembrandt, c. 1648). New York 1908, p. 21, no. 30 (as by Rembrandt). Valentiner 1909, no. 92 (as by Rembrandt). American Art News 1909, pp. 1–2, referenced p. 2 (as by Rembrandt). Cox 1909, p. 183 (as by Rembrandt). Holman 1910, p. 886 (as by Rembrandt). Waldmann 1910, p. 75 (as by Rembrandt). Wurzbach 1910, p. 410 (as a portrait by Rembrandt of the artist Jan Asselijn). Boston: 1910a , p. 1, no. 3 (as by Rembrandt). Boston 1910c, p. 46. Roberts 1912, p. 147 (as a painting by Rembrandt of a young man, signed and dated 1647). Valentiner 1914, p. 281 (as a portrait by Rembrandt of Jan van de Capelle). Hofstede de Groot 1915, p. 320, no. 763 (as a portrait by Rembrandt of a young painter, "once called Leonard Bramer," c. 1648). Valentiner 1921, p. 345 (as by Rembrandt, c. 1648). Meldrum 1922/23, p. 195, no. 256 (as by Rembrandt c. 1648). Wildenstein 1922, vol. 1, p. 145 (reprints the catalogue of Aved's November 1766 estate sale, in which the work is identified as a portrait by Rembrandt of Leonaert Bramer) and p. 208 (prints the inventory of Aved's state of June 16, 1766, in which the work appeared as *Le portrait de Brames par Rembrandt*). Van Dyke 1923, p. 78, illustrated plate XIV, fig. 53 (as by a pupil of Rembrandt, possibly Barent ["Bernaert"] Fabritius). Valentiner 1931, no. 97 (as a portrait by Rembrandt possibly of Carel Fabritius). Valentiner 1932, p. 203 and illustrated fig. 2 (as a portrait by Rembrandt possibly of Carel Fabritius, 1648). Benesch 1935, p. 39 (as by Rembrandt, noting suggestion that it portrays van de Cappelle). Bredius 1935, p. 11, no. 254, illustrated p. 539 (as by Rembrandt citing Valentiner's proposal that it is a portrait of Carel Fabritius). Bredius 1936, p. 11, no. 254, illustrated p. 539 (identically as in Bredius 1935). Valentiner 1941, p. 291, illustrated p. 288, fig. 14 (as a portrait by Rembrandt of van de Cappelle; here Valentiner takes back his 1932 identification of the subject as Carel Fabritius). Bredius 1942, p. 15, no. 254 (as by Rembrandt). Rosenberg 1948, vol. 1, p. 244 listed in the concordance, under Bredius no. 254 (with parentheses indicating Rosenberg's doubts about the painting's authenticity). Pittsburgh 1949, p. 124, no. 57 (and plate LVII in vol. III) (as by a pupil of Rembrandt). Rosenberg 1964, p. 371, section A, under Bredius no. 254 (as part of a list of works rejected by Rosenberg in this revised edition of his 1948 publication). Bauch 1966, p. 48, under Bredius no. 254 (as part of a list of works rejected by Bauch, who notes that the work is by a Rembrandt pupil "between Fabritius and the early Maes," c. 1648; citing Valentiner's outdated identification of the subject as Carel Fabritius). New York 1968, pp. 270–73, illustrated (without a specific attribution, but leaning toward the possibility of Barent Fabritius's authorship). Gerson 1969, p. 568, no. 254, illustrated p. 539 (as by a pupil of Rembrandt, perhaps Constantijn van Renesse or Barent Fabritius). Roscam Abbing 1987, pp. 97–99, no. 10, illustrated no. 52 (as a portrait of Samuel van Hoogstraten, c. 1649, possibly by a Dordrecht painter, perhaps Jan van Hoogstraten). Munhall 1988, pp. 17–18, no. 28 (as attributed to Rembrandt [the text notes the existing questions about its authorship and makes a comparison to Barent Fabritius]). Roscam Abbing 1989, p. 18, fig. 14 (as a portrait by a follower of Rembrandt possibly of Samuel van Hoogstraten). Sumowski 1983, vol. 4 (c. 1989), p. 2956, no. 1956, illustrated p. 3023 (as by an anonymous member of the Rembrandt school closer to C.D. van Renesse than to Barent Fabritius, c. 1650). Van Thiel 1992, p. 32 (visible in a reproduced photograph of the 1898 exhibition, Room 28, wall A), p. 34 (as no longer by Rembrandt), and illustrated p. 84. Sanger 1998, pp. 287, 289 (illustrated), 426 (as by a follower of Rembrandt). New York 2004, p. 128 (as by a follower of Rembrandt; previous editions of this publication list the painting [p. 120] with a Rembrandt attribution, but discuss in the text its probable authorship by a pupil or imitator). Bailey 2006, p. 15 (as by a follower of Rembrandt). Saltzman 2008, pp. 145–46, 159–63 (as by a follower of Rembrandt). Quodbach 2009, p. 234 (as by a follower of Rembrandt).

NOTES

1   Credit and thanks go to Dorothy Mahon, Paintings Conservator at The Metropolitan Museum of Art, who examined and cleaned this painting this past summer and who correctly observed for the first time these parts of the painting. Until then, the work had always been discussed as an image of a man drawing (whether with brush, pencil, or pen) on the paper that he holds. The presence of the brushes on the table, the manner in which he holds the album, and the thin lines of the image indicate that he is not drawing on it but painting on a canvas or panel we do not see.

2   On this subject, see Chapman and Woodall 2010, and Chapman 2005.

3   For the Paris sale of 1766, see the provenance section below and Wildenstein 1922, vol. 1, p. 145. Van Dyke 1923; although Van Dyke illustrates the painting with an attribution to Barent Fabritius, in his discussion on p. 78, he concludes that the assignment (based on comparison with another work by Barent, still assigned to him but now identified as *William van der Helm and His Family*, in the Rijksmuseum) is tentative, noting

that the work is "an excellent portrait."

4 See Scallen 2004, pp. 283–99.

5 Unpublished treatment report held by the Curatorial Department of The Frick Collection.

6 The first to publish the Frick painting as such (since Van Dyke in 1923) was Rosenberg 1948, vol. 1, p. 244, in the concordance, listed under Bredius no. 254. (See annotated references below.)

7 The following, in addition to Van Dyke, placed the painting in or around Barent Fabritius's oeuvre (or between Barent and the early work of Nicolaes Maes, in the case of Bauch): Pittsburgh 1949, p. 124; Bauch 1966, p. 48; New York 1968, pp. 270–73; Gerson 1969, p. 568; Munhall 1988, p. 17. The work is not consistent with others currently attributed to Barent, however, and this painter's oeuvre is as yet too ill defined to allow a sound judgment. The Frick painting shares characteristics with other works that have been tentatively connected to Gerbrand van den Eeckhout (*Portrait of a Man Seated in a Chair*, Lehman Collection, The Metropolitan Museum of Art, New York, and the pendants in the collection of the Duke of Westminster) and to Carel Fabritius (*Girl with a Broom*, National Gallery of Art, Washington, D.C.).

8 The catalogue of the J-A-J Aved sale of 1766 listed the work (no. 34) as a portrait by Rembrandt of Leonaert Bramer. Inscriptions on the former (but not original) stretcher and lining canvas that also identify the picture as a portrait of Leonaert Bramer are thought to date from Aved's ownership (Valentiner 1931, no. 97). Following universal dismissal of the Bramer identification, which seemed to rest on comparison with an etching after a lost portrait of Bramer, the seascape painter Jan van de Cappelle became the most popular hypothesis, this based on his inventory, which listed untraced portraits of him by Rembrandt and Hals (see References above). In 1931 and 1932 Valentiner considered Carel Fabritius to be the sitter, while still recognizing Rembrandt as the painter, but by 1941 reverted to his earlier van de Cappelle identification. The most recent proposal, made by M. Roscam Abbing in 1987 and 1989 (Roscam Abbing 1987, pp. 97–99), carries the most weight: on the basis of comparison with a drawn self-portrait in Munich by the Dordrecht native Samuel van Hoogstraten, he has proposed that this celebrated Rembrandt pupil, artist, and theorist is the subject of the Frick portrait. The resemblance in the full cheeks, wide nose, soft lips, and long locks of dark hair ending in curls is striking. However, other images of van Hoogstraten, like his *Self-Portrait in a Window* of 1644 (Bredius Museum, The Hague), do not bear such a strong resemblance. As Roscam Abbing (1989, p. 18) indicates, this appealing identification must remain a hypothesis.

9 De Winkel 2006, p. 159, writes that such hats begin to appear in Dutch portraits in 1645. Close comparisons for the other parts of the costume can be found in the *Portrait of a Man Seated in a Chair*, dated c. 1640–50, and tentatively attributed to Gerbrand van den Eeckhout (Lehman Collection, The Metropolitan Museum of Art) and Rembrandt's portrait of Gerard de Lairesse of the mid-1660s (also Lehman Collection, The Metropolitan Museum of Art).

10 According to Mahon, the X-radiographs show cusping on all four sides of the canvas, along with traces of the original stretcher, indicating that the canvas was only a few centimeters larger on the top, bottom, and left side and probably a bit more than that on the right side when it was primed by the artist in the studio. The dimensions listed in the 1766 Aved sale catalogue (41 pouces de haut; 31 de large, roughly 43 ½ x 33 inches) correspond to the size of the painting with the addition of the strip of canvas (still preserved at The Frick Collection), indicating that it was added by that date.

11 Munhall 1988, p. 17, notes the similar conception of this painting to Rembrandt's etched self-portrait of 1636, as well as to his *Self-Portrait at a Window* of 1648.

12 Visible in the X-radiographs and even on the surface of the painting, where the extended portions are visibly thinner and lighter.

13 Chapman 2005. On page 131, Chapman refers to the figure in Dou's *Man Writing by an Easel* of the 1630s as a conflation of painter and scholar.

14 Again, see Chapman and Woodall on the ways in which artists negotiated the relationship of the manual and intellectual aspects of their work in their depictions of painters at work and their discussion of this dichotomy of head and hand in relation to the Cartesian concept of mind and body: Chapman and Woodall 2010, especially p. 11.

15 Scallen 1998.

16 Chapman 2005, pp. 143–44.

17 Sluijter (2006, pp. 252–60) provides a historiographic review of discussions of the concept of emulation as it

applies to Dutch art and offers further insights derived from his study of seventeenth-century texts by and about artists. See also Luijten 1999, p. 76–77, who discusses Lampsonius's *Effigies* as a precursor to Van Dyck's Iconographia, in which the image of the painter as *pictor doctus* is propagated.

18 The Latin inscription below the portrait also stresses Floris's discipline and the labor he devoted to his craft. In Hendrik Hondius's revised and expanded edition of Lampsonius's book, the engraved portrait of Floris includes in the background the painting he is working on as well as the source material carefully held in his hands.

19 De Winkel (2006, p. 159) notes that contemporary hats of this nature were not prosaic, middle-class items, but accessories worn by wealthy individuals. See also Egbert Haverkamp-Begemann's discussion of the apparent affluence of the similarly attired man in *Portrait of a Man Seated in a Chair* (Lehman Collection, The Metropolitan Museum of Art) in New York 1998, pp. 148–51.

20 De Winkel (2006, p. 159 and p. 307, note 90) cites the unusualness of Rembrandt's choice to present himself in his work clothes, as there was no existing tradition for such depictions of painters.

21 Angel/Hoyle/Miedema 1942, p. 240.

22 Ibid. See also Sluijter 2000, p. 214.

23 Ibid.

24 Sluijter 2000, pp. 213–24.

25 Luijten 1999, p. 77.

5. Carel van der Pluym (1625–1672) *Old Woman with a Book*, c. mid-1650s

Oil on canvas

38 ⅝ x 30 ¼ inches (98.1 x 78.1 cm)

The Frick Collection, New York (16.1.99)

"Mr. Frick Buys a Rembrandt," reported *American Art News* in a front-page headline on October 21, 1916. Readers were informed that the picture—*Old Woman Reflecting over Her Reading*—joined three other paintings then attributed to the Dutch master in Henry Clay Frick's collection.[1] The painting was "said to have cost Mr. Frick about $250,000" and was installed in the grand gallery of his Manhattan mansion. While correct in identifying Frick as the purchaser, the journal had inflated the purchase price. Archival documents confirm that the collector had authorized the transfer of $202,446.22 from his Bankers Trust account to Morgan, Harjes & Co., Paris. The sum was released to the painting's owner, Jules Porgès (1839–1921), a key figure in the South African diamond and gold mining industries.[2] An illustration accompanying the article depicts a seated elderly woman, her face wrinkled and her gaze pensive. She is dressed in a fur jacket, voluminous skirt, and turban-like headdress. A pair of round spectacles lays entwined in the three middle fingers of her left hand, which rests on a large bound volume. The black and white image does not convey the painting's luminous autumnal palette or its vigorous impasto.

Listed as *Woman with Bible* on the transaction voucher and in Frick's ledger of painting purchases, it was titled *Old Woman Meditating over Her Reading* in the historic Rembrandt exhibition of 1898 in Amsterdam,[3] and *La Mère de Rembrandt* in an engraving made after the painting by J. J. van den Berghe in 1788.[4] Such inconsistencies in the painting's title hint at past ambiguities about the picture's subject. Rembrandt frequently portrayed elderly subjects in his painted and printed works, as did some contemporary artists and several of his students. Rather than portraying a specific individual, the artist probably intended to convey an edifying message. Moralizing themes feature prominently in seventeenth-century Dutch images, with depictions of elderly women frequently used to portray negative stereotypes—greedy procuresses, wizened coquettes—or positive ones—models of piety and wisdom. The Frick sitter falls into the latter category and more specifically within a genre depicting old women with a book, often interpreted as the Bible. Nearing her life's end, she prepares for her eternal reward.[5]

A painting by Rembrandt today in the Rijksmuseum, Amsterdam, is probably the source for these images (fig. 1). Monogrammed and dated 1631, the small panel is traditionally described as Rembrandt's mother reading,[6] probably in the guise of the prophetess Hannah, who was childless until she gave birth in her old age to the prophet Samuel.[7] Rembrandt depicts the aged woman wearing a flowing mantle and a shimmering striped headdress. She is earnestly perusing a large volume containing what appears to be Hebrew letters. Typically portrayed as elderly and pious, Hannah is a possible interpretation for the Frick painting too. Both figures wear striped, turban-like head coverings, fanciful creations used by

Fig. 1. Rembrandt van Rijn (1606–1669), *Old Woman Reading a Book*, 1631, oil on panel, 23 ½ x 18 ¾ inches (59.8 x 47.7 cm), monogrammed and dated: *RHL 1631*, Collection Rijksmuseum, Amsterdam, inv. no. SK-A-3006

Cornelis Hofstede de Groot (1863–1930) in the accompanying catalogue,[10] the painting's authorship was doubted by some of the exhibition's critics.[11] Likewise, Rembrandt expert Abraham Bredius (1855–1946)—a contributor to and reviewer of the exhibition—questioned Rembrandt's role in the painting's execution.[12] Bredius found the hands poorly executed and the woman's head reminiscent of works by Rembrandt's pupil Nicolaes Maes (1634–1693) but declared the brilliant mix of colors in the woman's robe to be indisputably by the master. He ultimately advocated joint authorship by Rembrandt and his workshop.[13] The scholar would revise his judgment later, rejecting any contribution by Rembrandt to the canvas's production.

Frick, however, was unaware of any controversy when he acquired the picture with the assistance of Edward Brandus of Messrs. E. Gimpel & Wildenstein. In a letter to Frick on February 3, 1916, Brandus stated: "I have reasons to believe that a great portrait by Rembrandt painted during his best period 1655 to 1660 can be obtained . . . " The dealer wrote to Frick again on May 12, 1916, declaring that, "the picture is guaranteed by Bredius, Bode, Hofstede de Groot, Friedlander and Valentiner . . . "[14]—all respected authorities on the artist. Soon after Frick's purchase was publicized, he received a letter from Bredius denouncing it:

> I am sorry to read that you have bought Mr. Porgès "Rembrandt" *Old Woman with the Book*. This is certainly <u>not</u> a Rembrandt but by <u>Carel van der Pluym</u> one of his minor pupils. . . . The picture has been exhibited some years ago in Paris where <u>all</u> clever art critics <u>agreed</u> that it was <u>not</u> by Rembrandt. . . . I do not understand that M. de Wild did not warn you to buy that picture. Try to give it back![15]

Western artists to signify Old Testament figures.[8] Such "oriental" headdresses were largely inventions by Western artists who had little knowledge of the clothing worn by women of the Middle East. The Frick sitter's costume appears to be a whimsical amalgam of exotic accouterments—the banded turban—and the wintry trappings in which elderly women were customarily depicted.[9]

In addition to equivocation over the picture's subject, the canvas's attribution has been passionately debated since the Rembrandt exhibition held in Amsterdam in 1898. Ascribed to Rembrandt by

Enchanted with his painting and unwilling to heed Bredius's claims, the usually taciturn Frick retorted.

I did not make that purchase without first having Dr. de Wild thoroughly examine and pass on the picture. Since receipt of your letter I have had the picture again examined by Dr. de Wild, who is positive it is without doubt a Rembrandt. . . . To my mind it is one of the finest Rembrandts in existence, and every visitor to my gallery, without exception, pays particular attention to it and grows enthusiastic over it. Why you should have reached the conclusion you have without something to base it on, I am at a loss to know. We all make mistakes, but it seems to me this is a most glaring one on your part.[16]

Carel de Wild (1870–1922), a renowned conservator and occasional adviser to Frick, crafted a lengthy diatribe reproaching the notoriously combative Bredius and reaffirming the canvas's authenticity:

When approximately do you think your studies will end, if, after thirty years of ceaseless toil you cannot distinguish the work of a great master like Rembrandt from that of his minor pupil? For this is what you call Carel van der Pluym. . . . The general technical execution, the broad sweeping brush work, the fat impasto, the wonderfully expressive face . . . the numerous details showing a master's treatment and finish in the wet paint suggest only one name and that is: Rembrandt![17]

Despite de Wild's protests and Frick's fervor for the picture, *Old Woman with a Book* is no longer included in Rembrandt's oeuvre. Bredius explained to Frick in a letter dated December 12, 1916, that a miscommunication between the eminent scholar Wilhelm Bode (1845–1929) and the restorer Alois Hauser (1831–1909) resulted in the painting's being incorrectly attributed to Rembrandt and sold to Frick as such.[18] Today, most scholars attribute the painting to Carel van der Pluym (1625–1672), an artist from a prominent Leiden family, who was Rembrandt's second cousin and probably his pupil and was rediscovered by Bredius.[19] Although his apprenticeship is undocumented, van der Pluym probably worked with Rembrandt between 1645 and 1648.[20] The

relationship was clearly amiable, with van der Pluym bequeathing 3000 guilders to Rembrandt's son, Titus, in his will of 1662 and later being named Titus's guardian in 1665. Van der Pluym's oeuvre also suggests an association between the two artists, with the younger painter continuing to work in Rembrandt's broad, rough manner even though this was considered old-fashioned after 1650 when the "fine style" practiced by Gerrit Dou (1613–1675) and Frans van Mieris (1635–1681) was preferred.[21] While van der Pluym's artistic output is small—probably owing to his successful civic career as Municipal Plumber of Leiden[22]—his talents were respected: he was accepted into the Leiden Guild of St. Luke in 1648, eventually becoming a master of the guild and later dean.

Bredius, struck by the similarities between the hands of the *Old Woman*—which he found clumsily painted and unlike any by Rembrandt—and those in a signed van der Pluym painting in another New York collection, urged Frick to compare the two pictures.[23] Although Frick apparently saw Dr. John E. Stillwell's *Old Man in a Fur Cap*, he resolutely chose to keep the *Old Woman*. Despite Frick's reluctance to accept an attribution to van der Pluym, the Stillwell painting, now in The Art Institute of Chicago, has many correspondences with the Frick work (fig. 2).[24] As Bredius noted, the hands in the two pictures are close in their general structure and the shape of the fingernails (figs. 3 and 4). Moreover, the methods used to create the paintings are comparable in the thick buildup of paint composing the forms and the small strokes meant to convey the highlights across the digits. Comparisons between the two paintings reveal analogous "blotchy description[s] of fur . . . [and] sketchy but labored drapery folds."[25] This is apparent in the fur composing the man's hat and the woman's jacket. Similar paint applications of longer, smooth strokes are found in the wrinkled foreheads of the figures, especially in the area just over the sitters' proper right eyebrow. Another common practice is the use of the back end of the brush to scratch into the painted surface, visible in the edges of both the woman's and man's tunic sleeves.

Besides affinities in painting technique, the pictures have comparable palettes. A recent correction of surface opacity in the varnish of the Frick canvas by

Fig. 2. Carel van der Pluym (1625–1672), *An Old Man in a Fur Cap*, 17th century, oil on cradled panel, 28 ¹/₁₆ x 21 ⁹/₁₆ inches (71.3 x 54.8 cm), signed: *Karel.van d[...]*, The Art Institute of Chicago, Bequest of Chester D. Tripp, 1988.265

Fig. 3. *Old Woman with a Book* (detail)

Fig. 4. Carel van der Pluym (1625–1672), *An Old Man in a Fur Cap* (detail), 17th century, oil on cradled panel, 28 ⁷/₁₆ x 21 ⁹/₁₆ inches (71.3 x 54.8 cm), signed: *Karel.van d[...]*, Bequest of Chester D. Tripp, acc. no.1988.265, The Art Institute of Chicago.

Dorothy Mahon of The Metropolitan Museum of Art enhanced the canvas's rich palette of ocher, russet, and crimson hues found also in the Chicago picture.[26] The slightly warmer appearance of the Chicago panel is probably due to its aged and somewhat yellowed varnish. Moreover, both artists illuminate their images in a similar manner: entering from the upper left of the picture, a concentrated radiance highlights the sitter's face, hands, and book before diffusing

across the darkened wall behind the figure's proper left shoulder.

Recent X-radiographs taken of the Frick painting provide further information about the canvas's development. The presence of a small head belonging to an unrelated composition can be seen near the old woman's chin (fig. 5). This partial figure, oriented horizontally under the surface of the *Old Woman*, is from a composition painted under the surface of the Frick picture. Although possibly composed by the creator of the *Old Woman*, it is more likely from an earlier composition, dating perhaps even before the seventeenth century. The recycling of old canvases was fairly common since the cost of such materials was substantial. In this instance, however, it makes the X-radiograph challenging to interpret because of the overlapping densities of lead white paint. In addition to the overlay of compositional elements, strokes of a randomly applied second priming were used to cover the earlier composition. The X-radiograph shows that alterations took place as the composition evolved. For example, changes were made to the contour of the turban. This is apparent when one compares the X-radiograph of the *Old Woman*'s headdress with the finished work. A close inspection of the painting's surface shows that there is also a change in the proper left arm of the chair, whose position was adjusted somewhat in the work's final paint layers, and one can see the artist's initial sketch through the thinly painted background.

Numerous similarities between the Frick canvas and the signed van der Pluym panel in Chicago, in addition to its affinities to other works ascribed to the artist, make an attribution to him plausible. The striking range of technique in the canvas—meticulous and smooth in the face, spontaneous and heavily impastoed along the sleeves—suggests that the Frick *Old Woman* was painted by someone familiar with Rembrandt's early and late styles, as van der Pluym

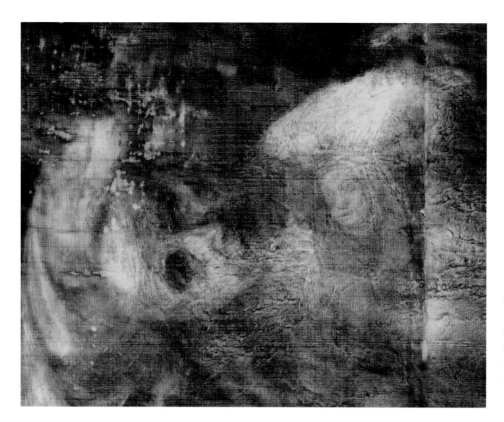

Fig. 6. *Old Woman with a Book*, detail of X-radiograph, Sherman Fairchild Center for Paintings Conservation, The Metropolitan Museum of Art

would have been. Van der Pluym painted the *Old Woman* between 1648 and 1659, the dates of his earliest and latest known works. A date toward the end of van der Pluym's activity—approximately the mid-1650s—seems most likely for the Frick canvas.[27]

M.I.

Provenance
[Catharina van der Pluym until her death in 1670.★ Count Thomas De Fraula (1647–1738), his sale July 21, 1738, Brussels (presumed to be lot 311).] Jan Pilaer and Nicolas François Joseph Beeckmans, Antwerp, probably by 1782. [Leith, Edinburgh. Ross, Edinburgh].★★ Charles Sedelmeyer (1837–1925), Paris; Jules Porgès (1839–1921), Paris by 1894; purchased in 1916 through Edward Brandus, Paris, by Henry Clay Frick for $202,446.

★ I. H. van Eeghen proposed that the Frick painting is by van der Pluym and identical to one described in the February 17, 1671, inventory of Catharina van der Pluym, the artist's aunt. While this identification

cannot be completely dismissed, the vague description makes it difficult to prove. See Van Eeghen 1977a, pp. 6–13. The work is described as "Een out besje, dat sit en leest" Catharina van der Pluym's inventory of 1671. The painting is published in the Getty Provenance Index as item 15 from Archival Documents N-2049 (Pluym).

★★ The Leith and Ross collections are listed only in the pedigree described by Edward Brandus in his letter of April 22, 1916, to Henry Clay Frick, contained in TFC/FARL Archives.

Exhibitions
École des Beaux-Arts, Paris, *Portraits de femmes et d'enfants*, 1897, no. 167, lent by Jules Porgès. Stedelijk Museum, Amsterdam, *Rembrandt-Tentoonstelling*, 1898, no. 71, lent by Jules Porgès.

References
July 21, 1738 sale, *Schilderyen, Grave de Fraula*, contained in G. Hoet, *Catalogus of naamlyst van schilderyen*, vol. 1, Gravenhage: P. G. van Baalen, 1752, p. 545, lot no. 311 [traditionally presumed to be this painting, artist not listed]. Michel 1894, vol. 2, pp. 22, 239 (as by Rembrandt). Paris 1897, p. 48, no. 167 (as by Rembrandt). Sedelmeyer 1898, p. 156, illustrated no. 138 (as by Rembrandt). Amsterdam 1898, no. 71 (as by Rembrandt). Hofstede de Groot 1898,

no. 24, illustrated (as by Rembrandt). Bredius 1899, pp. 191–98 (Bredius cites aspects of Rembrandt and students [such as Nicolaes Maes] in this work). Bode and Hofstede de Groot 1897–1905, vol. 5 (1901), p. 198, illustrated no. 392 (as by Rembrandt). Valentiner 1908, p. 560, illustrated p. 331 (attributed to Rembrandt but described as "unfinished"). American Art News 1916, p. 1, illustrated page 2 (as by Rembrandt). Hofstede de Groot 1916, p. 186, no. 320a (Hofstede de Groot notes; "If this was identical with a picture . . . in the collection of J. Porgès, Paris . . . it was not an original by Rembrandt"). Valentiner 1921, p. 125 (as probably by Nicolaes Maes). Martin 1921, pp. 30–34 (as by van der Pluym). Bode 1923, pp. 3–5 (revises his previous attribution to Rembrandt calling it doubtful). Van Dyke 1923, p. 143 (tentatively assigned to van der Pluym. Brusse 1926, pp. 93–94. Bredius 1931, pp. 241–64, illustrated p. 245, no. 5 (as by van der Pluym). Thieme-Becker 1933, Leipzig: E. A. Seemann, p. 164 (as by van der Pluym). Pittsburgh 1949, vol. 2, illustrated plate 60 (as by School of Rembrandt). New York 1968, pp. 249–51, illustrated (as by van der Pluym). Van Eeghen 1977a, vol. 64, pp. 6–13 (as by van der Pluym). Adams 1984, pp. 427–41, illustrated p. 434, fig. 12 (as by van der Pluym). Sumowski 1983, vol. 4 (c. 1989), pp. 2361–84 (as by van der Pluym). Van Thiel 1992, pp. 11–93, illustrated. Scallen 2004, pp. 141–44, 149, 257, 272, 276, 352 N39, 370 N44, illustrated fig. 33. Vogelaar and Korevaar 2005; illustrated p. 213, fig. 152. De Winkel 2006.

NOTES

1   American Art News 1916, p. 1, illustrated p. 2. The article identified the three other paintings in Frick's collection, all then ascribed to Rembrandt: *Portrait of Rembrandt by Himself*, *The Polish Rider*, and *Portrait of an Artist*. Frick's new acquisition was installed between Frans Hals's *Portrait of a Man* and Anthony Van Dyck's *Portrait of Marchesa di Brignole Sale* (now titled *Portrait of a Genoese Noblewoman*). I would like to thank Colin B. Bailey, Esmée Quodbach, and Louisa Wood Ruby for their thoughtful suggestions to this entry.

2   For documentation regarding Henry Clay Frick's purchase of this painting, see Henry Clay Frick Art Collection Files and Henry Clay Frick Papers, Series I: Art Files, both in The Frick Collection/Frick Art Reference Library Archives. I am indebted to Sally Brazil, Susan Chore, and Julie Ludwig of the Frick Art Reference Library (TFC/FARL) Archives for their collegiality and assistance with all the archival material cited in this essay.

3   The catalogue was published in French; thus the title was given as *Vielle Femme méditant sur sa lecture*. Amsterdam 1898, no. 71.

4   Van den Berghe is noted as having made an engraving after the picture in Edward Brandus's letter to Frick of April 22, 1916, in the Henry Clay Frick Art Collection Files, TFC/FARL Archives, although Brandus incorrectly lists the artist's name as van "der" Berghe. The engraving's title is given in the painting's entry in New York 1968, p. 249.

5   For a detailed discussion of the elderly figure in seventeenth-century Dutch art, see Anouk Janssen's essay in Vogelaar and Korevaar 2005, pp. 53–66.

6   For more on the Rijksmuseum's panel, see ibid., no. 17, pp. 110–13. As Vogelaar notes, the identification of the Rijksmuseum panel's subject as Rembrandt's mother is based on eighteenth-century accounts that noted a similarity to a model featured in several etchings by Rembrandt. John Smith published the painting as Rembrandt's mother in 1836, perpetuating the identification; see Smith 1836, p. 186, no. 592.

7   The story of the prophetess Hannah can be found in the Old Testament Books of Samuel, also known as the First and Second Books of Kings. The subject of the painting is identified as Hannah ("La Prophètesse Anne") as early as 1867 in the sale catalogue of the collection of the Count of Schönborn, Château de Pommersfelden (May 17, 1867), no. 97. Christian Tümpel identifies the model posing as Hannah as Rembrandt's mother in Tümpel 1993, cat. 76, p. 401, illustrated on p. 59. Members of the Rembrandt Research Project find the interpretation of Hannah plausible but are skeptical about Rembrandt's mother as the model. See Stichting Foundation Rembrandt Research Project; Corpus 1982, entry A37, pp. 351–57.

8   For more on Rembrandt and his followers' interpretation of such attire, see De Winkel 2006, pp. 252, 255, 262–70.

9   Anouk Janssen discusses traditional associations of warm clothing with elderly figures in her essay "The Iconography of Old Age and Rembrandt's Work," pp. 53–66, in Vogelaar and Korevaar 2005. For the iconography of old women wearing fur and its associations with old age, see p. 7.

10 See Amsterdam 1898, no. 71.

11 For example, Jan Veth (1864–1925), a noted artist and critic, expressed doubts that the *Old Woman* was by the Dutch master when reviewing the mammoth undertaking. See P. J. J. van Thiel's discussion of Veth's critical responses to the exhibition and other contemporary commentaries in van Thiel 1992, pp. 46–47.

12 It is interesting to note in the context of the current exhibition that Frits Lugt became acquainted with Abraham Bredius in 1901. Introduced by a friend of Lugt's father, the illustrious scholar gave the young man a test on the paintings in the Mauritshuis. Impressed by the precocious boy's enthusiasm and knowledge, Bredius presented Lugt to numerous scholars and collectors. For more about their relationship, see Reitsma 1997, pp. 33–44.

13 Although Bredius declined to give a firm attribution for the painting, he dated it to about 1650. Bredius 1899, p. 194. See also Catherine B. Scallen's discussion of the painting's reception at the 1898 exhibition in Scallen 2004, pp. 149–50.

14 Brandus's letters to Frick are contained in the Henry Clay Frick Art Collection Files, TFC/FARL Archives.

15 Bredius to Frick, October 19, 1916, Henry Clay Frick Art Collection Files, TFC/FARL Archives. "M. de Wild" to whom Bredius refers, is Carel Frederik Louis de Wild, an artist and restorer, who worked for Knoedler & Co., Frick's primary dealer. A brief biography is published in Thieme-Becker 1942, p. 558.

16 Frick to Bredius, November 21, 1916, Henry Clay Frick Art Collection Files, TFC/FARL Archives. Bredius replied in a letter of December 12, 1916, that when the painting was exhibited in Paris in 1897 he, Cornelis Hofstede de Groot, Joseph Otto Kronig, and Wilhelm Martin all agreed it was not by Rembrandt. Bredius ends his letter: "For 30 years I have constantly seen, seen again and studied *all* the works by Rembrandt. I discovered many of them—e.g. your *Polish Rider*—and I *know* that your picture *is certainly not by* Rembrandt, and all our best authorities *agree* with me!" Bredius wrote to Frick again on December 15, 1916, noting that Bode had said that he was relieved that Bredius did not accept the "so-called Rembrandt of Porgès." Henry Clay Frick Art Collection Files, TFC/FARL Archives.

17 See de Wild's protracted (five pages typed) retort to Bredius on February 6, 1917. Exceedingly pleased with de Wild's letter, Frick wrote to congratulate him in a letter dated February 14, 1917: "Your letter of February 6th to Dr. Bredius is a masterpiece. I would like to watch the old expert's [?] countenance while he was reading it. I am sure you have left him nothing to stand on." Henry Clay Frick Art Collection Files, TFC/FARL Archives.

18 Hauser intended to confirm that the canvas was an authentic seventeenth-century work and not a modern imitation; Bode mistook Hauser's remark to mean that the canvas was in fact executed by Rembrandt and conveyed this to Porgès, the painting's owner. In 1926 Marie-Joseph Brusse published this exchange, confirming Bredius's account. See Brusse 1926, pp. 93–94. My deepest thanks to Yvette Bruijnen for her help translating the Dutch texts cited in this essay.

19 See Bredius 1931, pp. 241–64.

20 As noted by Liedtke 1995, p. 114.

21 For more on the artist, see Werner Sumowski's biographic summary in Sumowski 1983, pp. 2361–62. I. H. Van Eeghen published additional archival material on van der Pluym in Van Eeghen 1977a, pp. 6–13.

22 Carel van der Pluym was made a member of the Council of Forty in Leiden in 1664.

23 In a letter dated October 19, 1916, Bredius noted, "the hands are exactly like those on van der Pluym's picture of the Stillwells." Henry Clay Frick Art Collection Files, TFC/FARL Archives.

24 Archival correspondence confirms that Stillwell invited Frick to see his picture and a reply from Frick indicates his willingness to visit Stillwell at his 9 West 49th Street address; no documentation exists describing Frick's reaction to the Stillwell painting. A second note from Stillwell thanks Frick for showing him his collection. See Stillwell's letters to Frick of February 24, 1917, and May 4, 1918, and Frick's to Stillwell of February 26, 1917, in Henry Clay Frick Papers, Series II: Correspondence, TFC/FARL Archives.

25 This is Walter Liedtke's apt description of van der Pluym's style when comparing the Chicago picture with another in The Metropolitan Museum of Art's collection—*Man in Armor (Mars?)*, acc. no. 71.84— which may have been painted by van der Pluym. See Liedtke 1995, pp. 112–15.

26 The Frick Collection is indebted to Conservator Dorothy Mahon of The Metropolitan Museum of Art's Sherman Fairchild Paintings Conservation Center for the treatment and technical study of this painting. Her work included the removal of a waxy covering from the canvas's surface and the correction of small surface defects. I am grateful to her for discussing her findings with me.

27 This dating is also in keeping with those paintings by van der Pluym that Sumowski finds related to the Frick canvas.

III. *Henry Clay Frick as a Collector of Rembrandt's Prints and Drawings*

In a letter of August 23, 1912, Charles Carstairs of M. Knoedler & Co. mentioned to his client Henry Clay Frick, seemingly in passing, that he had recently toured Windsor Castle and seen the collection of drawings held there.[1] This reference to the Windsor drawings may not in fact have been incidental but a possible effort to encourage Frick to start thinking about forming his own collection of works on paper. Two months later, in a letter of October 29, the dealer informed Frick that, while Knoedler had no paintings of interest to him at that time, the firm had enjoyed "a very satisfactory summer," purchasing on joint account with P. & D. Colnaghi's of London about 600 drawings from the British collector John Postle Heseltine (1843–1929).[2] Six days earlier *The New York Times* had announced this sale in a brief notice with the headline "$1,000,000 Is Paid for 600 Drawings" and the subheading, "Rembrandts unequaled." The text lauded the Rembrandt drawings in the collection as its finest treasures and rated them superior to those held "even in the great museums." Carstairs, familiar as he was with his client's collecting interests and tastes and perhaps aware of the *Times*'s coverage, continued in his letter to Frick, "It is a very big transaction, comprising about 600 drawings of all schools, but I do not think it would especially appeal to you in its entirety. You might, however, like the collection of Rembrandts—about 78 in number. There are also three wonderful Holbein drawings, in colour, and a wonderful Dürer. All of these would be interesting, framed and hung up in your new house."[3]

Ten months passed before Frick would purchase any of these drawings. In that period, Pierpont Morgan died and World War I began, two events that drastically changed the market of European works of art as it concerned Frick. Public sales of other drawings from Heseltine's enormous collection had also taken place in these months: in May 1913 *The New York Times* reported the sale of two of Heseltine's drawings by Rembrandt at auction in Amsterdam,

citing their high prices, which averaged over $3,750 apiece.[4] Against this backdrop, in October 1913 Frick purchased six of the Heseltine drawings acquired by Knoedler and Colnaghi for a little over $21,000, coming in just under the Amsterdam average with three works by Gainsborough and three attributed to Rembrandt—artists who were both already well represented in his collection of paintings.[5]

Frick had been acquiring works on paper, among them fine works by Jean-François Millet (1814–1875) and other nineteenth-century artists from the early days of his life as a collector for display in his Pennsylvania home, Clayton.[6] These he bequeathed to his descendants, many eventually becoming part of the collection of the Frick Art & Historical Center in Pittsburgh.[7] In 1913, with his new mansion on Fifth Avenue in construction and discussion about its decoration ongoing, he had to consider anew the place that works on paper would have in his collection and in his future museum at a time when, as Charles Ryskamp noted in 2003, the collecting of Old Master works on paper in America was still in its infancy.[8] As Carstairs well knew, Frick was a collector who would have no interest in keeping albums or boxes filled with large quantities of prints and drawings, as had Pierpont Morgan, who in 1909 purchased 1,400 drawings from the British collector Charles Fairfax Murray, or Cornelius Vanderbilt, who bequeathed his collection of 670 Old Master drawings to The Metropolitan Museum of Art in 1890. Frick would want them on view like his contemporaries H. O. and Louisine Havemeyer, who hung their prints and drawings by Degas, Cassatt, Whistler, Rembrandt, and others on designated walls of their home.[9] Similarly, Frick's solution was to install his works on paper in the smaller spaces of the second floor of his New York mansion, creating, as Susan Grace Galassi has written, "a small parallel collection of the masters whose paintings hung in the formal rooms on the main floor."[10] Frick thus looked for a comparable degree of formality in the prints and drawings he acquired. He was not interested in small sketches, figure studies, or other preparatory works with the telltale signs of workshop use. As a collector of masterpieces who had posterity in view, he wanted pristine sheets by major artists featuring compositions worthy of finished paintings.

Frick's 1913 purchase marked the beginning of this new phase of his collecting of works on paper. Those six sheets, although not all finished drawings intended by their makers for contemporary collectors, bear worked-out compositions rather than studies of individual figures or motifs. Of the three drawings attributed to Rembrandt, two are autonomous, finished sheets that present fully articulated landscapes. The third—a depiction of the Old Testament scene *Isaac Blessing Jacob*—features summarily rendered figures, but its heavy washes define the space and light and complete the composition and earned it a place on the cover of a 1907 catalogue of Rembrandt drawings in Heseltine's collection.[11] These three works by Rembrandt are wildly different in style: the rapid, thick, ink-laden lines of the *Landscape with Cottage, Trees, and Stream* contrast with the lighter touch and more even hatching of the *Farmyard with Trees and Figures* (by far the most expensive in this sale) as well as with the extremely broad, painterly handling of *Isaac Blessing Jacob*. We now know that the last two are most likely not by Rembrandt, but such disparity was then understood as a reflection of an experimental and temperamental artist whose technique changed with his mood and personal circumstances. As the scholar Malcolm Bell wrote of Rembrandt's drawings in 1899, "The style is as diverse as the material."[12] This romantic notion, although flawed, points to Rembrandt's very real ability and inclination to vary the thickness of his lines and the amount of ink he applied to his pen, even in a single sheet, and to experiment with the exposure of the bare paper and application of washes for different effects of light and shadow.

As Carstairs must have hoped when he wrote to Frick in August 1912, the collector made a practice of buying works on paper from Knoedler. From this point on, his interest lay primarily in prints, by definition finished compositions created for an audience. On April 30, 1915, Frick purchased an engraving by

Dürer and two famous etchings by Rembrandt: *The Three Trees* and the so-called *Goldweigher's Field*.[13] Again, Frick chose complex compositions and images very different in character from one another, though certainly by the same hand. Both landscapes exhibit Rembrandt's mastery of the medium, in diverse ways. Leaving much of his copper plate untouched and, with the greatest economy of means, deftly scratching through its coating with his needle, he produced the spare and luminous landscape of *The Goldweigher's Field*. An equal assuredness and effectiveness of line is present in *The Three Trees*, but here Rembrandt emphasizes the lushness of the trees and the underbrush (in which two lovers meet at lower right) and the dramatic light effects caused by the rapidly passing clouds and piercing rays of sunlight—achieved by dense hatching across large areas of the plate and brilliantly placed passages of light.

Henry Clay Frick and his family were installed in their new Manhattan home by 1915. In that year and the one that followed, Frick would dramatically enlarge his collection, primarily through his major acquisition of sculpture and decorative arts from the estate of the late Pierpont Morgan. He would also purchase in May 1916, among other paintings, *Old Woman with a Book*, then attributed to Rembrandt (now to Carel van der Pluym). That he also continued to expand his holdings of works on paper, rather than reserving all his funds for paintings and three-dimensional objects, suggests the importance he attached to this other part of his collection. Less than two weeks after the van der Pluym acquisition, and more than a year after his purchase in 1915 of three pastels and a set of twelve etchings by James McNeill Whistler—the nineteenth-century heir to Rembrandt's experimental approach to printmaking—Frick acquired six more etchings by the master: two portraits, three landscapes, and *St. Francis Praying beneath a Tree* (a landscape as much as a religious subject). As before, these prints, along with the Van Dyck portrait print of Pieter Brueghel, two Dürer engravings, and two prints by Charles Meryon from his *Etchings of Paris* series that also formed part of this sale, came from Knoedler in carved frames, ready to be hung. The invoice documenting the sale also noted the quality of the impressions and condition of the sheets, which included first states of the *Portrait of Clement de Jonghe* and *Landscape with White Paling*.[14]

Frick's final acquisition of works on paper—three large religious prints by Rembrandt purchased for $42,000 a month before Frick's death in November 1919[15]—suggests that his ambitions as a collector of prints and drawings had grown and might have continued in this vein had his life not come to an end. Although fewer in number than his paintings, sculpture, or decorative arts objects, the prints and drawings Frick acquired were significant purchases and, considering that they were assembled in separate sales and over the course of only six years, represent a concentrated effort on his part to build this area, which most likely he intended from the start to leave to the Collection.

Rembrandt's personal significance to Frick is often noted. With his addition of fourteen works on paper (eleven of which bear unquestioned attributions to the master) to his ensemble of paintings by the master, the collector strove to build his holdings of this artist's magnificently expansive oeuvre. Edwin Bechtel's introduction to the 1951 catalogue of works on paper in The Frick Collection was incorrect in noting that Frick had his spectacular impression of the *Ecce Homo* on his desk in late 1919: that print and the other two purchased that year, *The Hundred Guilder Print* and a first state of *The Three Crosses*, did not arrive at 1 East 70th Street until a couple of months after Frick's death. The collector's special preference for Rembrandt is, however, evident.[16] As Frick had begun his collecting of Old Master paintings with Rembrandt, so he began his collecting of Old Master works on paper with him.

The prints and drawings by Rembrandt were among the oldest works on paper that Frick collected (the Dürer and Van Dyck are the only examples he acquired that predate them) and, as such, they connected him with the longer tradition of collecting prints and drawings. The etched portrait of the silversmith Jan Lutma that Frick purchased in 1916 in fact bears the mark of the famous French collector and dealer Pierre-Jean Mariette (1694–1774),[17] while all the prints Frick acquired would have been made by Rembrandt with such an audience in mind— "amateurs" (*liefhebbers* in Dutch) who prized prints as well as drawings by contemporary artists and masters of the past, keeping them both in albums and in frames on the walls of their homes.

J.S.

NOTES

1   Carstairs to Frick, August 23, 1912, TFC/FARL Archives. Thanks are due to the Frick archivists Sally Brazil, Susan Chore, and Julie Lugwig for keeping such material in so superbly organized and easily searchable form.

2   Carstairs to Frick, October 29, 1912, ibid.

3   Ibid.

4   "Rembrandts at High Prices," in *The New York Times*, May 29 1913.

5   Invoice from M. Knoedler & Co. to Henry Clay Frick, October 11, 1913, TFC/FARL Archives. Frick already owned the *Portrait of a Young Artist*, now attributed to a follower of Rembrandt (purchased 1899), Rembrandt's *Self-Portrait* (purchased 1907), and *The Polish Rider* (purchased 1910), and Gainsborough's portraits of Mrs. Charles Hatchet (purchased 1903) and Frances Duncombe (purchased 1911).

6   Charles Ryskamp, "Preface," in New York 2003, p. xix.

7   Ibid. Before and after 1913, Frick would acquire works on paper destined for his other estates and left to his descendants, as well as gifts for friends and associates. The reproductive prints after Sir Joshua Reynolds, Sir Thomas Lawrence, George Romney, and John Hoppner in The Frick Collection were acquired by Frick (in 1905, 1908, 1914, and 1916), but not bequeathed by him to the museum. Instead they descended through the family and were given to the Collection in the 1970s and 1980s.

8   Charles Ryskamp, "Preface," in New York 2003, p. xx. See Bailey 2006 on the construction of Frick's home and the motivations behind his collecting practices in these years.

9   New York 1993, p. 191, fig. 36, shows a photograph of the Havemeyer home with a group of matted works on paper on the wall.

10 Galassi 2000, pp. 285–92, p. 286.

11 London 1907.

12 Bell 1899, p. 130. Across the Atlantic, in 1913, Frits Lugt, then an employee of the Amsterdam auction

house Frederik Muller & Cie, quoted Bell's line in writing about other Rembrandt drawings from the Heseltine collection that would appear at auction there in May of that year.

13 Invoice dated May 31, 1916 (noting both the April 30, 1915, and May 31, 1916, sales) from M. Knoedler & Co. to Henry Clay Frick, TFC/FARL Archives.

14 Ibid.

15 Invoices dated March 8, 1917, and February 13, 1920 (noting the date of sale as November 3, 1919), from M. Knoedler & Co. to Henry Clay Frick, TFC/FARL Archives.

16 Edwin DeT. Bechtel, "Foreword," in New York 1951, n.p. The arrival of these three prints in February 1920 is documented by the invoice dated February 13, 1920 (noting the date of the decision of sale as November 3, 1919), from M. Knoedler & Co. to Henry Clay Frick and two letters from M. Knoedler & Co. to the estate of H. C. Frick of January 31, 1920 (noting that the special frames for the prints were not yet ready) and of February 13, 1920 (confirming their delivery). See also the deposition by Charles Carstairs of January 9, 1920, and a letter of January 8, 1920, from William Ivins, Jr., to H. C. McEldowney, Esq., Pittsburgh, All TFC/ FARL Archives.

17 New York 2003, p. 196.

IV. *Checklist of Works on Paper by Rembrandt van Rijn in The Frick Collection*

Landscape with Three Trees, 1643

Etching, drypoint, and burin
(single state); image: 8 ⅜ x 11 inches
(21.3 x 27.9 cm); sheet: 8 ⅞ x 11 ⅜ inches
(22.5 x 28.9 cm)
1915.3.28

Christ Preaching (The Hundred Guilder Print), c. 1643–49

Etching, drypoint, and burin
on dark cream-colored Japanese
wove paper (state II of II)
image: 11 x 15 ⅜ inches
(27.9 x 39.1 cm); sheet: 12 ¼ x 16 ¾
inches (31.2 x 42.6 cm)
1919.3.33

Cottage with a White Paling, 1648?

Etching (state I of III)
image. 5 ⅛ x 6 ¼ inches (13.0 x 15.9 cm),
sheet: 5 ½ x 6 ½ inches (14 x 16.5 cm)
1916.3.27

Landscape with Three Gabled Cottages, 1650

Etching and drypoint (state III of III)
image: 6 ⅜ x 8 inches (16.2 x 20.3 cm);
sheet: 6 ½ x 8 ¼ inches
(16.5 x 21 cm)
1916.3.30

The Goldweigher's Field, 1651

Etching and drypoint (single state)
image: 4 ¾ x 11 ⁹⁄₁₆ inches (12.1 x 32 cm); sheet: 5 ⅜ x 13 ⅛ inches
(13.7 x 33.3 cm)
1915.3.31

Clement de Jonghe, 1651

Etching (state I of VI)
image: 8 ⅛ x 6 ⅜ inches
(20.7 x 16.2 cm); sheet:
8 ¾ x 6 ¾ inches (22.2 x 17.2 cm)
1916.3.36

Christ Crucified between Two Thieves (The Three Crosses), by 1653

Drypoint and burin on vellum
(state I of V)
sheet (cut inside the plate mark):
15 ⅛ x 17 ⅝ inches (38.4 x 44.8 cm)
1919.3.34

Christ Presented to the People (Ecce Homo), by 1655

Drypoint on cream-colored Asiatic
wove paper (state II of VIII)
sheet (cut inside the plate mark):
15 ¼ x 17 ⅞ inches (38.7 x 45.4 cm)
1920.3.32

Jan Lutma the Elder, 1656

Etching and drypoint (state II of III)
sheet (cut inside the plate mark):
7 ⅞ x 5 ⅞ inches (20 x 14.9 cm)
1916.3.37

St. Francis Praying Beneath a Tree, 1657

Drypoint, etching, and burin
(state II of II)
sheet (cut inside the plate mark):
7 ⅟₁₆ x 9 ⅝ inches (17.9 x 24.5 cm)
1916.3.35

v. *Frits Lugt: A Passion for Rembrandt*

Like Henry Clay Frick (1849–1919), who was once described as "a little too enthusiastic about pictures, but not enough to hurt,"[1] Frederik Johannes Lugt (1884–1970) felt a deep fervor for art beginning in his youth. He recalled, "When I was about thirteen, the passion for painting and the old masters awoke in me."[2] Both men would create collections filled with works of the highest quality by myriad artists, yet Rembrandt would remain a favorite of each.

Between September 8 and October 31, 1898, a historic exhibition of works by Rembrandt was held at the Stedelijk Museum in Amsterdam to celebrate the coronation of Queen Wilhelmina of the Netherlands (1880–1962). To say that the occasion was memorable for the fourteen-year-old Amsterdammer familiarly known as Frits would be an understatement. From the age of ten, Lugt spent much of his time in the Rijksmuseum copying from and studying its collection, perhaps inspired by his early desire to be an artist. At age twelve he became a regular visitor to the Rijksprentenkabinet, where he spent countless hours exploring its precious works on paper. Eventually the young man would embark on a catalogue of the drawings in the collection, since none existed. He would catalogue 955 drawings before other events commanded his attention.[3] Years later, as an accomplished art historian, Lugt would extol the importance of drawing after masterworks and studying art firsthand advising that, "The art historian should have more than book-learning in his youth. His subject is art, and he must have some of the artist's productive, not to say creative, mind."[4]

The precocious young man was creative, indeed, and crafted an eloquent biography on the artist, complete with his own drawings made after the master's major works. The painstaking project occupied him for eighteen months between the ages of fourteen and sixteen and resulted in a manuscript that comprised 162 handwritten pages, including a chronology, index, and list of recommended literature.[5] In 1899, the year

following the Rembrandt exhibition, Lugt purchased his first work by the Dutch master—an etching of Lieven van Coppenol—at an Amsterdam auction for about three guilders.[6] That same year, the forty-nine-year-old Henry Clay Frick would make his first Rembrandt purchase—a painting titled *Portrait of a Young Artist*, now attributed to a follower of Rembrandt, acquired from Arthur Tooth & Sons for $38,000.[7]

This painting, along with three others that either Frick, or later, the Frick trustees would acquire as Rembrandt, were included in the 1898 Amsterdam show and are on view in the present exhibition.[8] These works include *The Polish Rider*, *Nicolaes Ruts*, *Portrait of a Young Artist*, and *Old Woman with a Book* (now attributed to Rembrandt's cousin and likely pupil, Carel van der Pluym). One wonders what the clever youth—a future expert on Rembrandt who would become thoroughly familiar with the complicated issues of Rembrandt attribution—thought of each of these paintings when he saw them in the 1898 display. Although primarily a collector of drawings and prints, Lugt acquired paintings occasionally, his chief interest being Dutch pictures from the seventeenth century. Among these treasured works, a small Rembrandt *Self-Portrait* on copper—acquired by Lugt in 1924 and now in the Nationalmuseum, Stockholm—held special appeal. Like Frick, Lugt had a predilection for landscapes, seascapes, and portraits. In addition, the younger collector enjoyed still lifes, animal pieces, and church interiors but shunned scenes of ribald activities or those with erotic overtones.[9]

Lugt's early admiration for Dutch and Flemish works, and especially for those by Rembrandt, would shape the course of his life. He withdrew from secondary school in 1901 to accept a position at the auction house of Frederik Muller & Cie in Amsterdam. The opportunity proved vital to his training, sharpening his visual skills and exposing him to the oeuvres of many artists.[10] Through his employment at the auction house, Lugt encountered several of the works on paper in the current exhibition, then available on the market. Lugt left Frederik Muller in 1915. Financially secure after his marriage in 1910 to Jacoba Klever (1888–1969), a coal magnate's daughter, and no longer prohibited from purchasing art as an employee of Frederik Muller, the seasoned connoisseur could now begin to build his personal collection.

Perhaps it is not surprising based on his early labors in the Rijksmuseum's print room that works on paper form the greatest part of the Lugt collection. Today the Lugt Collection/Fondation Custodia's holdings consists of 30,000 prints and 7,000 Old Master drawings by Dutch, Flemish, Italian, French, Danish, German, and English artists. These prized sheets are stored in leather-bound albums, following the practice of eighteenth-century connoisseurship. The works are categorized by subject except for those by Rembrandt, his school, Van Dyck, and Rubens, which are kept in special albums.[11] Drawings by seventeenth-century Dutch artists make up the majority of the collection; of these, twenty-one are attributed to Rembrandt. All of Lugt's accepted drawings by the Dutch master were purchased between 1919 and 1954, but he would acquire works by those in Rembrandt's circle throughout his life.[12] Lugt acquired his first Rembrandt etching as an adult in 1917, eventually compiling a nearly complete set of prints by the artist.[13] Besides drawings and etchings by Rembrandt and his associates, and the collection of paintings already mentioned, Frits and Jacoba built up an exceptional assemblage of portrait miniatures, books, artists' letters, and other prints and drawings all now in the care of the Fondation Custodia in Paris. The Lugts eschewed traditional installations that grouped works by discipline and school, finding these bland and uninspired. Instead, they created ensembles of paintings, decorative arts, and furniture, intended to be visually pleasing and as faithful as possible to historic examples.

As Frits Lugt tells us, a great collector does not necessarily accumulate vast amounts of works but makes shrewd selections ("Il ne s'agit pas d'amasser, mais de choisir").[14] The connoisseur's own practices adhered to this philosophy, engendering a collection filled with works of exceptional quality as confirmed by the current exhibition. One of the most impressive sheets—and a favorite of Lugt's—is Rembrandt's luminous drawing *Interior with Saskia in Bed*, c. 1640–42. Masterfully employing ink, wash, and chalk to mimic the effects of light and shadow, the artist captures an intensely private moment, which probably depicts his wife Saskia's lying-in following the birth of one of their children. A striking assortment of Rembrandt etchings from the Fondation Custodia is on view as well. Of these, a group of self-portraits present the artist in a variety of costumes, settings, and humors and create a powerful dialogue with the Frick's painted *Self-Portrait*.

Although Rembrandt was his favorite artist, Lugt eagerly collected drawings by the master's mentors, contemporaries, students, and followers. Beautiful in their own right, they also provide insight into the development of seventeenth-century Dutch art. Lugt understood the significance of Rembrandt's relationships with his fellow artists, noting, "We find...few traces of intimate friendship with other painters, excepting his pupils."[15] Among the artists from Rembrandt's circle featured in the present exhibition are Pieter Lastman (1583–1633); Ferdinand Bol (1616–1680), Lambert Doomer (1624–1700), Gerbrand van den Eeckhout (1621–1674), Govert Flinck (1615–1660), Samuel van Hoogstraten (1627–1678), Philips Koninck (1619–1688), Jan Lievens (1607–1674), and Nicolaes Maes (1634–1693). From brief sketches to highly finished drawings, these superb sheets include portraits, genre scenes, figure and animal studies, landscapes, and biblical episodes. They reveal influences from and responses to Rembrandt and in some cases may have inspired the master's own work.

A fascinating juxtaposition in the Frick installation compares Lambert Doomer's *Old Farm at the Edge of a Wood*, acquired by Lugt in 1964, with Rembrandt's bucolic *Cottage near the Entrance to a Wood*, signed and dated 1644, on loan from the Robert Lehman Collection of The Metropolitan Museum of Art. Doomer most likely owned Rembrandt's drawing, which has long been assumed to have served as the younger artist's model. Recent scholarship examines the possibility of Doomer's landscape being the inspiration for Rembrandt's work.[16] This notion is intriguing, especially since Lugt must have seen

Rembrandt's drawing when it passed through the Frederik Muller auction house in 1913.

Lugt is renowned today not only as a savy collector but also as a brilliant scholar. His *Marques de collections de dessins et d'estampes* (published in 1921) and four-volume *Répertoire des catalogues de ventes publiques intéressant l'art ou la curiosité* (published between 1938 and 1987) are still standard reference tools demonstrating Lugt's capacity for meticulous archival scholarship, while publications like the 1913 sales catalogue of the John Postle Heseltine collection reveal Lugt to be an astute connoisseur. In his *Wandelingen met Rembrandt in en om Amsterdam* of 1915, Lugt literally retraces Rembrandt's steps, mapping his promenades in Amsterdam and its surrounding areas. This remarkable work was the result of scrupulous studies of the artist's landscape drawings and prints. A recognized expert of Dutch and Flemish works on paper, Lugt made major contributions to this field, frequently cataloguing entire collections, including those in the Louvre, the Bibliothèque nationale de France, and the École des Beaux-Arts, Paris. Somewhat ironically, he chose not to catalogue his own works, preferring to leave this task to others.

When reminiscing on his life's work, Lugt likened his role to that of a guardian, who had the "stubborn patience to produce a number of works which, while not themselves works of art, have helped to defend the cause of true works of art."[17] He praised the meritorious efforts of discerning past collectors and patrons "to whom we are indebted for the survival of all the art treasures which now crowd our museums and private galleries" adding, "We can do no more for their blessed memories than express, in a general way, our deep gratitude for the work they have so well done."[18] This simple statement could serve as a fitting epitaph for Lugt himself and his remarkable contributions. As the numerous publications devoted to Frits Lugt and his role as a collector and expert on Rembrandt note, the connoisseur's date of death—July 15, 1970—occurred on the same month and day as Rembrandt's birth. For a kindred spirit who devoted his life to analyzing Rembrandt's works, copying his pencil strokes, and retracing his footsteps, this seems a fitting last act.

M.I.

NOTES

1   As quoted in Bailey 2006, pp. 10–11. I would like to thank Louisa Wood Ruby and Joanna Sheers, my colleagues at the Frick Art Reference Library and The Frick Collection, respectively, for their generous advice on this essay.

2   As quoted in Reitsma 1997, p. 34.

3   Numerous publications discuss Frits Lugt as a collector and expert on Rembrandt. The most recent addition is Peter Schatborn's essay "Frits Lugt and Drawings by Rembrandt" in Schatborn 2010. Other notable works on this topic include Mària van Berge-Gerbaud's preface in Hinterding 2008, pp. 7–14; her essay "Frits Lugt et Rembrandt" in Van Berge-Gerbaud 1997, pp. XI–XVI; as well as Reitsma 1997, pp. 33–44, and Reitsma 2002, pp. 11–38.

4   Lugt 1943, p. 182.

5   Reitsma 1997, p. 33.

6   As noted in Schatborn 2010.

7   *Paintings and Other Works of Art Owned by Henry C. Frick* (Red Book), folio 49, Henry Clay Frick Art Collection Files, TFC/FARL Archives.

8   For a complete listing of paintings in the exhibition, see Amsterdam 1898.

9   As discussed in Reitsma 2002, p. 30.

10   Ibid., pp. 17–18.

11   Ibid., p. 38.

12   As noted by Mària van Berge-Gerbaud in her preface to Schatborn 2010.

13   Mària van Berge-Gerbaud in Hinterding 2008, p. 8.

14   As quoted in Paris 1994, p. 9.

15   Lugt 1915, p. 162.

16   See Schatborn 2010.

17   Reitsma 1997, p. 34.

18   Lugt 1943, pp. 180–81.

VI. *Checklist of Works on Paper from the Frits Lugt and Robert Lehman Collections*

Rembrandt van Rijn (1606–1669)

Self-Portrait, Frowning: Bust, 1630

> Etching (state II of III [IV]); image: 2 ¹³⁄₁₆ x 2 ⁷⁄₁₆ inches
> (7.2 x 6.1 cm); sheet: 2 ¹⁵⁄₁₆ x 2 ½ inches (7.4 x 6.3 cm)
> Fondation Custodia, Collection Frits Lugt, Paris
> (Inv. No. 1548)

Rembrandt van Rijn (1606–1669)

*Sheet of Studies: Head of the Artist, a Beggar Couple,
Heads of an Old Man and Woman, etc.*, c. 1632

> Etching (state II of II); image: 3 ¹⁵⁄₁₆ x 4 ¹⁄₁₆ inches
> (10.0 x 10.4 cm); sheet: 4 ³⁄₁₆ x 4 ¼ inches
> (10.6 x 10.9 cm)
> Fondation Custodia, Collection Frits Lugt, Paris
> (Inv. No. 1571)

Rembrandt van Rijn (1606–1669)

*Self-Portrait in a Cap and Scarf with the Dark Face:
Bust*, 1633

> Etching (state II of II); image: 5 ³⁄₁₆ x 4 ¹⁄₁₆ inches
> (13.2 x 10.3 cm); sheet: 5 ⅜ x 4 ³⁄₁₆ inches
> (13.7 x 10.7 cm)
> Fondation Custodia, Collection Frits Lugt, Paris
> (Inv. No. 4109)

Rembrandt van Rijn (1606–1669)
Self-Portrait with Raised Sabre, 1634

Etching, with touches of burin (state II of II), retouched by
a later hand with brush and gray ink
image: 4 ¹³⁄₁₆ x 4 inches (22.2 x 10.1 cm);
sheet: 4 ⅞ x 4 inches (12.4 x 10.2 cm)
Fondation Custodia, Collection Frits Lugt, Paris (Inv. No. 3885)

Rembrandt van Rijn (1606–1669)
Self-Portrait Wearing a Soft Cap: Full Face, Head Single
("aux trois moustaches"), c. 1635

Etching (single state)
image: 1 ¹⁵⁄₁₆ x 1 ¹¹⁄₁₆ inches (5.0 x 4.3 cm);
sheet: 4 ¹⁄₁₆ x 3 ⅛ inches (10.4 x 7.9 cm)
Fondation Custodia, Collection Frits Lugt, Paris (Inv. No. 616)

Rembrandt van Rijn (1606–1669)
Self-Portrait with Saskia, 1636

Etching (state II of III)
image: 4 ¹⁄₁₆ x 3 ¾ inches (10.4 x 9.5 cm);
sheet: 4 ½ x 4 inches (11.5 x 10.2 cm)
Fondation Custodia, Collection Frits Lugt, Paris (Inv. No. 3861)

Rembrandt van Rijn (1606–1669)
Self-Portrait Leaning on a Stone Sill, 1639

Etching (state I of II)
image: 8 ¹⁄₁₆ x 6 ⁷⁄₁₆ inches (20.5 x 16.4 cm);
sheet: 8 ³⁄₁₆ x 6 ⁹⁄₁₆ inches (20.8 x 16.7 cm)
Fondation Custodia, Collection Frits Lugt, Paris (Inv. No. 3990)

Rembrandt van Rijn (1606–1669)

Self-Portrait Etching at a Window, 1648

    Etching, drypoint, and burin on Japanese paper (state II of V)
    image: 6 ³⁄₁₆ x 5 inches (15.7/15.8 x 12.8 cm);
    sheet: 6 ³⁄₈–6 ½ x 5 ³⁄₁₆ inches (16.2–16.5 x 13.2 cm)
    Fondation Custodia, Collection Frits Lugt, Paris (Inv. No. 4087)

Rembrandt van Rijn (1606–1669)

*Bearded Man, in an Oriental Fur Cap and Robe: The Artist's
Father*, 1631

    Etching and burin (state III of IV)
    image: 5 ¼ x 5 ⅛ inches (14.6 x 13.0 cm);
    sheet: 6 ⁹⁄₁₆ x 5 ⁹⁄₁₆ inches (16.8 x 14.2 cm)
    Fondation Custodia, Collection Frits Lugt, Paris (Inv. No. 5242)

Rembrandt van Rijn (1606–1669)

*The Artist's Mother Seated at a Table, Looking Right:
three-quarter length*, c. 1631

    Etching and burin (state II of III); framed by four lines
    in pen and black ink
    5 ⅞ x 5 ⅛ inches (15.0 x 13.0 cm) (cropped inside the plate mark)
    Fondation Custodia, Collection Frits Lugt, Paris (Inv. No. 1569)

Rembrandt van Rijn (1606–1669)

The Artist's Son, Titus, c. 1656

    Etching, with plate tone on Japanese paper (single state)
    image: 3 ⅞ x 2 ¾ inches (9.8 x 7.0 cm);
    sheet: 4 ¹⁄₁₆ x 3 inches (10.4 x 7.6 cm)
    Fondation Custodia, Collection Frits Lugt, Paris (Inv. No. 2076)

Rembrandt van Rijn (1606–1669)

Three Studies of an Old Man, c. 1635

   Pen and brown ink, light brown prepared paper (laid down)
   6 ⅞ x 6 ⁵⁄₁₆ inches (17.4 x 16.0 cm)
   Fondation Custodia, Collection Frits Lugt, Paris
   (Inv. No. 1922)

Rembrandt van Rijn (1606–1669)

Woman with a Child Frightened by a Dog, c. 1635–36

   Pen and brown ink, heightened with white under the arm of the
   child and framed by four lines in pen and brown ink
   4 ¹⁄₁₆ x 4 inches (10.3 x 10.2 cm)
   Fondation Custodia, Collection Frits Lugt, Paris (Inv. No. 5155)

Rembrandt van Rijn (1606–1669)

Three Studies of a Woman with a Child in Her Arms, c. 1630s
(probably c. 1637–38)

   Pen and brown ink, some rubbing with a finger
   7 ⅜ x 6 inches (18.7 x 15.3 cm)
   Fondation Custodia, Collection Frits Lugt, Paris (Inv. No. 4904)

Rembrandt van Rijn (1606–1669)

A Woman Having Her Hair Combed, c. 1637–38

   Pen and brown ink on light brown paper
   4 ³⁄₁₆ x 3 ⅞ inches (10.7 x 9.8 cm)
   Fondation Custodia, Collection Frits Lugt, Paris (Inv. No. 805)

Rembrandt van Rijn (1606–1669)

Woman Leaning on a Window Sill, dated c. 1638

Pen and brown ink, brown wash, in some places applied with half-dry brush and/or rubbed with a finger, on light brown prepared paper
6 ¹¹/₁₆ x 4 ¹⁵/₁₆ inches (17.0 x 12.5 cm)
Fondation Custodia, Collection Frits Lugt, Paris (Inv. No. 288)

Rembrandt van Rijn (1606–1669)

Seated Old Man, late 1630s

Pen and brown ink, brown wash, some lines drawn in the wet ink with end of the brush with some corrections in white and three framing lines in pencil
6 ⁷/₁₆ x 5 ¹/₁₆ inches (16.4 x 12.9 cm)
Fondation Custodia, Collection Frits Lugt, Paris (Inv. No. 4502)

Rembrandt van Rijn (1606–1669)

Two Women Teaching a Child to Walk and a Sketch of a Woman Seen from the Back, late 1630s

Pen and brown ink with brown wash and some corrections in white on light brown prepared paper
6 ⅜ x 5 ¾ inches (16.2 x 14.6 cm)
Fondation Custodia, Collection Frits Lugt, Paris (Inv. No. 5447)

Rembrandt van Rijn (1606–1669)

The Martyrdom of a Woman, c. 1640

Pen and brown ink with white wash on two pieces of paper
7 ¹¹/₁₆ x 10 ¹/₁₆ inches (19.5 x 25.6 cm)
Fondation Custodia, Collection Frits Lugt, Paris
(Inv. No. 5302)

Rembrandt van Rijn (1606–1669)
Interior with Saskia in Bed, c. 1640–42

    Pen and brown ink with brown and gray wash and some
additions in red and black chalk
5 ⁹⁄₁₆ x 6 ¹⁵⁄₁₆ inches (14.2 x 17.7 cm)
Fondation Custodia, Collection Frits Lugt, Paris
(Inv. No. 266)

Rembrandt van Rijn (1606–1669)
The Grain Mill "De Bok" on the Bulwark "Het Blauwhoofd,"
mid-1640s

    Pen and brown ink with brown wash (laid down)
4 ½ x 7 ¾ inches (11.6 x 19.8 cm)
Fondation Custodia, Collection Frits Lugt, Paris
(Inv. No. 5174)

Rembrandt van Rijn (1606–1669)
Woman with a Child on Her Lap, second half of the 1640s

    Pen and brown ink with brown wash applied with a half-dry
brush or finger and traces of framing lines in pen and brown ink
(partly cut)
6 ⅜ x 5 inches (16.2 x 12.8 cm)
Fondation Custodia, Collection Frits Lugt, Paris (Inv. No. 2143)

Rembrandt van Rijn (1609–1669)
A Woman Stealing from the Pocket of a Sleeping Drunkard,
c. 1650

    Pen and brown ink, heightened with white, framed by
four lines in brown ink (laid down)
4 x 5 ⅜ inches (10.1 x 13.6 cm)
Fondation Custodia, Collection Frits Lugt, Paris
(Inv. No. 5993)

Rembrandt van Rijn (1606–1669)
Landscape with a Bear Fighting with a Goat, after Titian,
c. 1650

Pen and brown ink, framed by four lines in pen and brown ink
on light brown paper (laid down)
8 x 11 ⁹⁄₁₆ inches (20.3 x 29.4 cm)
Fondation Custodia, Collection Frits Lugt, Paris
(Inv. No. 6584)

Rembrandt van Rijn (1606–1669)
The Prophet Elijah and the Angel in the Desert, early 1650s

Pen and brown ink, brown wash, rubbed with a finger,
with corrections in white
6 ¹¹⁄₁₆ x 6 ½ inches (17.0 x 16.5 cm)
Fondation Custodia, Collection Frits Lugt, Paris
(Inv. No. 3564)

Rembrandt van Rijn (1609–1669)
The Angel Leaving Manoah and His Wife, early 1650s

Pen and brown ink, partially rubbed with a finger or a dry brush
8 ³⁄₁₆ x 7 ¹⁄₁₆ inches (20.8 x 18.0 cm)
Fondation Custodia, Collection Frits Lugt, Paris
(Inv. No. 5803)

Rembrandt van Rijn (1606–1669)
Farmhouse and a Haystack, 1650s

Pen and brown ink, brown wash, put on some places with
half-dry brush or rubbed with a finger, corrections and accents
in white, on grayish brown paper (at the top a horizontal fold,
at the right a framing line in pencil, at the top right and left
repairs with newly inserted paper)
5 ⅝ x 10 ⅝ inches (14.3 x 27.0 cm)
Fondation Custodia, Collection Frits Lugt, Paris
(Inv. no. 302)

Rembrandt van Rijn (1606–1669)

Shah Jahan, Standing with a Flower and a Sword, c. 1656–61

Pen and brown ink with brown wash on Asiatic paper (mounted)
7 x 4 inches (17.8 x 10.1 cm)
Fondation Custodia, Collection Frits Lugt, Paris (Inv. No. 592)

Rembrandt van Rijn (1609–1669)

The Healing of the Mother-in-Law of Saint Peter, late 1650s

Pen and brown ink, brown wash, in some places rubbed with a
finger, heightened with white, framed by four lines in pen and
brown ink (backed/mounted)
6 ¼ x 7 ⁷⁄₁₆ inches (17.1 x 18.9 cm)
Fondation Custodia, Collection Frits Lugt, Paris (Inv. No. 5794)

Pieter Lastman (1583–1633)

Standing Mercury, 1620s

Red and white chalk on yellowish prepared paper
11 ⅛ x 8 ³⁄₁₆ inches (28.2 x 20.8 cm)
Fondation Custodia, Collection Frits Lugt, Paris
(Inv. No. 2000-T.6)

Jacob Pynas (1592/3–after 1650)

The Descent from the Cross, early 1630s

Pen and brown ink, rubbed in some places (arms and heads), on
light brown paper
7 ⅜ x 7 ½ inches (18.7 x 19 cm)
Fondation Custodia, Collection Frits Lugt, Paris (Inv. No. 6531)

Jan Lievens (1607–1674)

Portrait of Jan Francken, the Servant of Johan van Oldenbarnevelt, later 1640s or 1650s

Pen and brown ink (paper repaired below left and center; some areas have been damaged by the gallnut ink; laid down)
10 ¹⁵⁄₁₆ x 8 ⁹⁄₁₆ inches (22.8 x 21.8 cm)
Fondation Custodia, Collection Frits Lugt, Paris
(Inv. No. 2009)

Jan Lievens (1607–1674)

A Hilly Landscape with a Dilapidated House, probably 1660s

Pen and brown ink, framed by four lines in pen and dark brown ink
8 ¹³⁄₁₆ x 15 ¹⁵⁄₁₆ inches (22.4 x 40.5 cm)
Fondation Custodia, Collection Frits Lugt, Paris
(Inv. No. 896)

Jan Lievens (1607–1674) or Jan Andrea Lievens (1644–1680)

View in a Wood, 1660s

Pen and brown ink with brown wash, framed by four lines in pen and dark brown ink
9 ⅞ x 15 ⁹⁄₁₆ inches (25.1 x 39.5 cm)
Fondation Custodia, Collection Frits Lugt, Paris
(Inv. No. 4014)

Govert Flinck (1615–1660)

Landscape with a Willow Tree and a Building near a Stone Bridge, 1642

Pen and brown ink with gray, brown, and gray-brown wash, framed by three lines in pen and brown ink, the lower line, above the margin, also in pen and brown ink, traced in pencil
5 ¼ x 7 ¾ inches (13.4 x 19.8 cm)
Fondation Custodia, Collection Frits Lugt, Paris
(Inv. No. 2796)

Govert Flinck (1615–1660)
Sleeping Child, 1643

> Pen and brown ink with light brown wash, framed by
> four lines in pen and gray-brown ink
> 6 ½ x 5 ¹³⁄₁₆ inches (16.5 x 14.8 cm)
> Fondation Custodia, Collection Frits Lugt, Paris
> (Inv. No. 7368)

Govert Flinck (1615–1660)
Reclining Female Nude, 1640s

> Black and yellowish white chalk on blue paper
> 9 ¹³⁄₁₆ x 16 ¼ inches (24.9 x 41.2 cm)
> Fondation Custodia, Collection Frits Lugt, Paris
> (Inv. No. 2969)

Ferdinand Bol (1616–1680) (formerly attributed to Rembrandt)
Elijah Sleeping beneath a Tree, third quarter of the 1630s

> Pen and brown ink
> 3 ⅜ x 4 ½ inches (8.5 x 11.5 cm)
> Fondation Custodia, Collection Frits Lugt, Paris
> (Inv. No. 2526)

Ferdinand Bol (1616–1680)
The Angel Appearing to Hagar in the Desert, late 1630s

> Pen, brown and gray ink with gray wash
> 11 ½ x 7 ¼ inches (29.3 x 18.5 cm)
> Fondation Custodia, Collection Frits Lugt, Paris
> (Inv. No. 2529)

Ferdinand Bol (1616–1680)

View in the Dunes near Haarlem, 1640s

Black chalk with brown and gray wash
5 ¾ x 11 ½ inches (14.7 x 29.2 cm)
Fondation Custodia, Collection Frits Lugt, Paris
(Inv. No. 6009)

Gerbrand van den Eeckhout (1621–1674)

The Centurion of Capernaum Kneeling before Christ, later 1630s

Pen and brown ink with gray and brown wash, some lines in
black chalk, and corrections in white body color, framed by
three unruled lines in pen and brown ink and four ruled lines
in pen and black ink
7 ½ x 10 inches (19.0 x 25.5 cm)
Fondation Custodia, Collection Frits Lugt, Paris
(Inv. No. 5197)

Gerbrand van den Eeckhout (1621–1674)

Self-Portrait (?), 1647

Point of the brush in black and gray ink with black and
gray-brown wash over a sketch in black chalk, framed by
four lines in pen and black ink
10 ⅜ x 7 ⅞ inches (26.4 x 20.0 cm)
Fondation Custodia, Collection Frits Lugt, Paris (Inv. No. 854a)

Gerbrand van den Eeckhout (1621–1674)

The City Walls of Delft with the Mill called The Rose, c. 1645

Black chalk and gray wash, framed by four lines in pen and
dark brown ink
4 ¹⁵⁄₁₆ x 7 ½ inches (12.5 x 19.1 cm)
Fondation Custodia, Collection Frits Lugt, Paris
(Inv. No. 4445)

Gerbrand van den Eeckhout (1621–1674)
The Satyr and the Peasant, c. 1653

> Black and some red chalk with gray wash and watercolor in
> brown, brown-yellow, and pink, framed by four lines in pen
> and black ink
> 8 ½ x 9 ⅞ inches (21.7 x 25.1 cm)
> Fondation Custodia, Collection Frits Lugt, Paris
> (Inv. No. 9206)

Gerbrand van den Eeckhout (1621–1674)
Youth Smoking, 1650s

> Point of brush and brown ink with brown and some gray wash,
> framed by four lines in pen and brown ink
> 6 ¼ x 5 ⅞₆ inches (15.9 x 13.8 cm)
> Fondation Custodia, Collection Frits Lugt, Paris
> (Inv. No. 92)

Gerbrand van den Eeckhout (1621–1674)
Studies of a Dog Lying Down, 1650s

> Point of brush in brown ink with brown wash and four framing
> lines in pencil
> 11 ⅝₆ x 7 ¹³⁄₁₆ inches (29.4 x 19.9 cm)
> Fondation Custodia, Collection Frits Lugt, Paris (Inv. No. 5822)

Gerbrand van den Eeckhout (1621–1674)
View of Gorinchem, c. 1661–65

> Pen and brown ink and watercolor over a drawing in
> black chalk, partially traced in brown ink, with four framing
> lines in pen and brown ink and a second line at top in pen
> and brown ink, on two pieces of paper
> 7 ¹⁵⁄₁₆ x 14 ⅜ inches (20.1 x 36.5 cm)
> Fondation Custodia, Collection Frits Lugt, Paris
> (Inv. No. 93)

Gerbrand van den Eeckhout (1621–1674)
Hannah Presents Her Son Samuel to the High Priest Eli,
mid-1660s

Pen and brown ink with gray, black, and dark violet wash over
a sketch in black chalk, framed by four lines in pen and
dark brown ink
5 ¾ x 7 ⁷⁄₁₆ inches (14.7 x 18.9 cm)
Fondation Custodia, Collection Frits Lugt, Paris (Inv. No. 5303)

Gerbrand van den Eeckhout (1621–1674)
Designs for Title Pages in Polybius's Histories, c. 1669

Pen and brown ink with brown wash over traces
of black chalk and framing lines in pen and brown ink
(indented for transfer to copper plate)
left: 5 ¹³⁄₁₆ x 3 ¾ inches (14.8 x 9.6 cm);
right: 5 ¹³⁄₁₆ x 3 ⅞ (14.8 x 9.8 cm)
Fondation Custodia, Collection Frits Lugt, Paris
(Inv. Nos. 3556A/B)

Attributed to Carel Fabritius (1622–1654)
(formerly attributed to Rembrandt)
Rebecca and Eliezer at the Well, c. 1640–45

Pen and brown ink with brown and gray wash, heightened
with white body color over some lines in black chalk
(backed with Japanese paper)
7 ⁵⁄₁₆ x 11 ¹³⁄₁₆ inches (18.6 x 30.0 cm)
Fondation Custodia, Collection Frits Lugt, Paris (Inv. No. 9629

Samuel van Hoogstraten (1627–1678)
Death of the Virgin, c. 1645–50

Pen and brown ink with brown wash and additions of red and
black chalk and four framing lines in pen and brown ink
10 ³⁄₁₆ x 9 ¾ inches (25.8 x 24.8 cm)
Fondation Custodia, Collection Frits Lugt, Paris
(Inv. No. 1971-T.51)

Samuel van Hoogstraten (1627–1678)
Study of a Camel, 1640s

> Pen and brown ink with brown wash and, below, a framing line
> in pen and brown ink
> 3 ¹¹⁄₁₆ x 9 ½ inches (9.3 x 13.9 cm)
> Fondation Custodia, Collection Frits Lugt, Paris
> (Inv. No. 9027)

Samuel van Hoogstraten (1627–1678)
A Kitchen with a Boy Warming Himself at the Fire, c. 1648

> Pen and point of brush in brown ink with brown and gray wash
> 5 ⅜ x 6 ⁹⁄₁₆ inches (13.6 x 16.7 cm)
> Fondation Custodia, Collection Frits Lugt, Paris
> (Inv. No. 3739)

Samuel van Hoogstraten (1627–1678)
Title Page: The Muse Erato, 1678

> Pen and brown ink with brown wash over traces of black chalk
> and four framing lines in pen and brown ink (partly indented for
> transfer to copper plate; verso prepared with red chalk)
> 6 ¹⁵⁄₁₆ x 5 ⁵⁄₁₆ inches (17.7 x 13.5 cm)
> Fondation Custodia, Collection Frits Lugt, Paris (Inv. No. 5162)

Nicolaes Maes (1634–1693)
Seated Woman Scraping a Parsnip, c. 1655

> Point of the brush in brown ink, framed by four lines in pen
> and dark brown ink
> 4 ⅞ x 3 ⁵⁄₁₆ inches (12.4 x 8.4 cm)
> Fondation Custodia, Collection Frits Lugt, Paris
> (Inv. No. 863)

Nicolaes Maes (1634–1693)
Woman Embroidering, c. 1654–58

Red chalk, brown and reddish brown wash, with rounded framing
line at top applied with the point of the brush and brown ink
and traces of a framing line below in pen and dark brown ink
7 ¹⁵⁄₁₆ x 6 ⁷⁄₁₆ inches (20.2 x 16.4 cm)
Fondation Custodia, Collection Frits Lugt, Paris (Inv. No. 420)

Constantijn van Renesse (1626–1680)
A Road between Trees Leading to a Farmhouse, c. 1652–53

Pen and brown ink with brown wash, heightened with
white body color and framed by four lines in pen and
brown ink
8 ¾ x 13 inches (22.2 x 33 cm)
Fondation Custodia, Collection Frits Lugt, Paris
(Inv. No. 2222)

Philips Koninck (1619–1688)
Panoramic River Landscape, c. 1650–55

Pen and brown ink with brown and gray-brown wash
7 ⁹⁄₁₆ x 12 ⁵⁄₁₆ inches (19.3 x 31.3 cm)
Fondation Custodia, Collection Frits Lugt, Paris
(Inv. No. 1199)

Philips Koninck (1619–1688)
The Mocking of Christ, late 1650s/c. 1662

Pen, brush, brown ink, and brown wash with traces of
a framing line at top in pen and brown ink
6 ⅞ x 8 ⅞ inches (17.5 x 22.5 cm)
Fondation Custodia, Collection Frits Lugt, Paris
(Inv. No. 1970-T.34)

Philips Koninck (1619–1688)
River Landscape with a Town on the Horizon, c. 1660

Pen and brown ink with brown wash, watercolor,
and four framing lines in pen and brown ink (backed)
2 ¹⁵⁄₁₆ x 7 ¹¹⁄₁₆ inches (7.5 x 19.6 cm)
Fondation Custodia, Collection Frits Lugt, Paris
(Inv. No. 261)

Lambert Doomer (1624–1700)
View of Angers, 1646

Pen and brown ink with brown wash and gray, blue,
and green watercolor on ledger paper and four framing lines
in pen and black ink
9 ⁵⁄₁₆ x 15 ⅞ inches (23.7 x 40.4 cm)
Fondation Custodia, Collection Frits Lugt, Paris
(Inv. No. 5463)

Lambert Doomer (1624–1700)
Standing Donkey with a Saddle, c. 1645–46

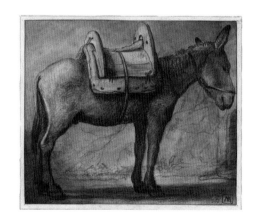

Black chalk with brown and gray wash and
four framing lines in pen and brown ink
5 ⅜ x 6 ⁵⁄₁₆ inches (13.6 x 16.1 cm)
Fondation Custodia, Collection Frits Lugt, Paris
(Inv. No. 1977-T.60)

Lambert Doomer (1624–1700)
View of Mönchengladbach, 1663

Black chalk with brown, gray, grayish-green, and ocher
watercolor and four framing lines in pen and black ink
9 ⁹⁄₁₆ x 15 ¹¹⁄₁₆ inches (24.3 x 39.8 cm)
Fondation Custodia, Collection Frits Lugt, Paris
(Inv. No. 5841)

Lambert Doomer (1624–1700)

View of the Godesburg and the Drachenfels, 1663

Pen and brown ink with brown and gray wash, framed by
four lines in pen and dark brown ink (lower line in brown ink,
left partly cut)
7 ¹¹⁄₁₆ x 11 ¼ inches (19.6 x 28.6 cm)
Fondation Custodia, Collection Frits Lugt, Paris (Inv. No. 2228)

Lambert Doomer (1624–1700)

Old Farm at the Edge of a Wood (after Rembrandt), c. 1658

Pen and brown ink, brown and reddish brown wash,
and traces of black chalk with some lines in red chalk
11 ¹¹⁄₁₆ x 17 ³⁄₁₆ inches (29.7 x 43.7 cm)
Fondation Custodia, Collection Frits Lugt, Paris
(Inv. No. 8236)

Also exhibited:

Rembrandt van Rijn (1606–1669)

Cottage near the Entrance to a Wood, 1644

Pen and inks ranging from light to dark brown with
brown washes, corrections in white (oxidized and partially
abraded), and touches of red chalk (in structures to the left
of the main cottage)
11 ¾ x 17 ¹⁵⁄₁₆ inches (29.9 x 45.5 cm)
The Metropolitan Museum of Art, New York,
Robert Lehman Collection, 1975 (1975.1.792)

Bibliography

Adams 1851. John Adams. "Diary," in *The Works of John Adams, Second President of the United States*, vol. 3. Boston: Charles C. Little and James Brown, 1851.

Adams 1984. Henry Adams. "If Not Rembrandt, Then His Cousin?," in *The Art Bulletin*, vol. 66, no. 3 (Sept. 1984): 427–41.

Alpers 1988. Svetlana Alpers. *Rembrandt's Enterprise: The Studio and the Market*. Chicago: University of Chicago Press, 1988.

American Art News 1908. "Old Masters at Union League," in *American Art News*, vol. 6, no. 13 (January 11, 1908): 1–8.

American Art News 1909. "Hudson-Fulton Memorial Exhibition," in *American Art News*, vol. 7, no. 35 (September 20, 1909): 1–2.

American Art News 1910. "Exhibitions," in *American Art News*, vol. 9, no. 8 (December 3, 1910): 1–2.

American Art News 1916. "Mr. Frick Buys a Rembrandt," in *American Art News*, vol. 15, no 2 (October 21, 1916): 1.

Amsterdam 1898. *Rembrandt: Collection des oeuvres du maître réunies à l'occasion de l'inauguration de S. M. la Reine Wilhelmine au Musée de la Ville à Amsterdam, 8 Septembre–31 Octobre 1898*, exh. cat. Stedelijk Museum, Amsterdam 1898.

Amsterdam 1913. *Dessins de Rembrandt de la collection J.P. Heseltine de Londres*. Amsterdam: Frederik Muller & Cie, May 27, 1913.

Angel/Hoyle/Miedema 1642/1996. Philips Angel. *Lof der Schilder-konst*. Leiden, 1642, translated by Michael Hoyle with an introduction and discussion by Hessel Miedema in *Simiolus*, vol. 24, no. 2/3 (1996): 227–58.

Art World 1917. "The Henry Clay Frick Collection," in *Art World*, vol. 1, no 6 (March 1917): 374–78.

The Athenaeum 1876. "The Private Collections of England: No. XXVIII.–Castle Howard: Low Country Schools," in *The Athenaeum: Journal of Literature, Science, the Fine Arts, Music, and the Drama*, no. 2554 (October 7, 1876): 468–70.

Bailey 1978. Anthony Bailey. *Rembrandt's House*. Boston: Houghton Mifflin, 1978.

Bailey 1990. Anthony Bailey. "A Young Man on Horseback," in *The New Yorker* (March 5, 1990): 45–77.

Bailey 1994. Anthony Bailey. *Responses to Rembrandt*. New York: Timken Publishers, 1994.

Bailey 2002. Colin B. Bailey. "Henry Clay Frick, Roger Eliot Fry, and Rembrandt's *Polish Rider*," in *The Frick Collection Members' Magazine* (spring/summer 2002): 10–12.

Bailey 2006. Colin B. Bailey. *Building The Frick Collection: An Introduction to Its House and Its Collections*. New York: The Frick Collection and Scala Publishers, 2006.

Bal 1991. Mieke Bal. *Reading Rembrandt: Beyond Word-Image Opposition*. Cambridge: Cambridge University Press, 1991.

Bal and Bryson 1992. Mieke Bal and Norman Bryson. "Some Thoughts on 'Semiotics and Art History,'" in *The Art Bulletin*, vol. 74, no. 3 (September 1992): 522–31.

Bauch 1933. Kurt Bauch. *Die Kunst des Jungen Rembrandt*. Heidelberg: C. Winter 1933.

Bauch 1966. Kurt Bauch. *Rembrandt: Gemälde*. Berlin: W. De Gruyter, 1966.

Baudiquey 1984. Paul Baudiquey. *La Vie et l'oeuvre de Rembrandt*. Paris: ACR Edition, 1984.

Bedaux and Ekkart 2000. Jan Baptist Bedaux and Rudi Ekkart, eds. *Pride and Joy: Children's Portraits in the Netherlands 1500–1700*, exh. cat. Haarlem: Frans Hals Museum; Antwerp: Koninklijk Museum voor Schone Kunsten, 2000.

Bell 1899. Malcolm Bell. *Rembrandt van Rijn and His Work*. London: G. Bell, 1899.

Benesch 1935. Otto Benesch. *Rembrandt. Werk und Forschung*. Vienna: Gilhofer & Ranschburg, 1935.

Benesch 1973. Otto Benesch. *The Drawings of Rembrandt*, vol. 5. London: Phaidon Press, 1973.

Berger 2000. Harry Berger, Jr. *Fictions of the Pose: Rembrandt against the Italian Renaissance*, Stanford: Stanford University Press, 2000.

Berlin, Amsterdam, and London 1991–92. *Rembrandt: The Master and His Workshop*, exh. cat. Berlin: Gemäldegalerie; Amsterdam: Rijksmuseum; London: National Gallery, 1991–92.

Białostocki 1969. Jan Białostocki. "Rembrandt's Eques Polonus," in *Oud Holland*, vol. 84 (1969): 163–76.

Białostocki 1984. Jan Białostocki. "A New Look at Rembrandt Iconography," in *Artibus et Historiae*, vol. 5, no. 10 (1984): 9–19.

Binstock 1999. Benjamin Binstock. "Rembrandt's Paint," in *RES: Anthropology and Aesthetics*, no. 36 (autumn 1999): 138–65.

Bikker 2002. Jonathan Bikker. "Drost's End and Loth's Beginnings in Venice," in *The Burlington Magazine*, vol. 144, no. 1188 (March 2002): 147–56.

Bikker 2005. *Willem Drost: A Rembrandt Pupil in Amsterdam and Venice.* New Haven and London: Yale University Press, 2005.

Bode 1883. Wilhelm von Bode. *Studien zur Geschichte der holländischen Malerei: Mit Facsimiles der Künstlerinschriften.* Braunschweig: F. Vieweg, 1883.

Bode 1909. Wilhelm von Bode. *Great Masters of Dutch and Flemish Painting.* Translated by Margaret L. Clark. London: Duckworth and Co., and New York: C. Scribner's Sons, 1909.

Bode 1923. Wilhelm von Bode. "Der 'Rembrandt-Forschung' in Gefahr?," in *Der Kunstwanderer*, vol. 5 (1923): 3–5.

Bode and Hofstede de Groot 1897–1905. Wilhelm von Bode and Cornelis Hofstede de Groot. *Rembrandt: Beschreibendes Verzeichniss seiner Gemälde.* 8 vols. Paris: Charles Sedelmeyer, 1897–1905.

Bolten and Bolten-Rempt 1978. J. Bolten and H. Bolten-Rempt. *The Hidden Rembrandt.* Translated by Danielle Adkinson. Oxford: Phaidon, 1978.

Bomford, et al. 2006. David Bomford, et al. *Art in the Making: Rembrandt.* London: The National Gallery, 2006.

Bonafoux 1985. Pascal Bonafoux. *Rembrandt: Self-Portraits.* New York: Rizzoli, 1985.

Boston 1910a. *Loan Exhibition of Pictures from the Collection of Henry C. Frick: December 1 to December 15, 1910.* Boston: Museum of Fine Arts, 1910.

Boston 1910b. "Frick Art Collection Exhibit Opens Today," in *Boston Post* (Friday, December 2, 1910).

Boston 1910c. "Mr. Henry C. Frick's Pictures," in *Museum of Fine Arts Bulletin*, vol. 8, no. 48 (December 1910): 46–47.

Bredius 1891. Abraham Bredius. "Noch eine kleine Dosis anti-Lautnerianum," in *Der Sammler*, vol. 13, no. 7 (July 1, 1891): 73–75.

Bredius 1897. Abraham Bredius. "Onbekende Rembrandts in Polen, Galicie en Rusland," in *De Nederlandsche Spectator*, vol. 25 (June 19, 1897): 197–99.

Bredius 1899. Abraham Bredius. "Kritische Bemerkungen zur Amsterdamer Rembrandt-Ausstellung," in *Zeitschrift für bildende Kunst*, vol. 34 (1898/99): 161–68, 191–98.

Bredius 1931. Abraham Bredius. "Karel van der Pluym, neef en leerling van Rembrandt," in *Oud Holland*, vol. 48 (1931): 241–64.

Bredius 1935. Abraham Bredius. *Rembrandt Gemälde.* Vienna: Phaidon, 1935.

Bredius 1936. Abraham Bredius. *The Paintings of Rembrandt.* Vienna: Phaidon, 1936.

Bredius 1942. Abraham Bredius. *The Paintings of Rembrandt.* New York: Oxford University Press, 1942.

Broos 1974. B. P. J. Broos. "Rembrandt's Portrait of a Pole and His Horse," in *Simiolus*, vol. 7, no. 4 (1974): 192–218.

Broos 1991a. B. P. J. Broos. "Bredius, Rembrandt en het Mauritshuis!!!," in *Bredius, Rembrandt en het Mauritshuis: een Eigenzinnig Directeur Verzamelt*, exh. cat. The Hague: Mauritshuis, 1991.

Broos 1991b. B. P. J. Broos. "Het Mysterie van de Poolse Ruiter," in *Vrij Nederland*, vol. 52, no. 49 (December 1991): 52–56.

Broos 1993. B. P. J. Broos. *Intimacies and Intrigues: History Painting in the Mauritshuis.* The Hague: Mauritshuis, 1993.

Brown 1989. Christopher Brown. "Re-appraising Rembrandt," in *Sotheby's Preview* (November/December 1989): 6–9.

Brown 1992. Christopher Brown. "Lastman, Lievens, and Bredius. Amsterdam, Leiden, and The Hague," in *The Burlington Magazine*, vol. 134, no. 1069 (April 1992): 268–72.

Brunet 2009. Lynn Brunet. "Homage to Freemasonry or Indictment: The Cremaster Cycle," in *PAJ: A Journal of Performance and Art*, vol. 31, no. 1 (January 2009): 98–112.

Brusse 1926. M. J. Brusse. *Knoeierijen in den Schilderijenhandel.* Rotterdam: W. L. & J. Brusse's Uitgevers-Maatschappij, 1926.

Bruyn 1984. Joshua Bruyn. "Review, *Gemälde der Rembrandt-Schüler, I* by W. Sumowski," in *Oud Holland*, vol. 98 (1984): 146–62.

Bühler 1949. Hans E. Bühler. *Reiterbilder in der europäischen Malerei.* Zurich: Atlantis, 1949.

Buijsen 1990. Edwin Buijsen. "The Battle against the Dollar…," in *Great Dutch Paintings from America*, exh cat. Edited by Ben Broos. The Hague: Mauritshuis; San Francisco: The Fine Arts Museums of San Francisco, 1990.

Burroughs 1907. Bryson Burroughs. "Two Recent Loans," in *The Metropolitan Museum of Art Bulletin*, vol. 2, no. 7 (July 1907): 126.

Campbell 1970. Colin Campbell. "Rembrandt's 'Polish Rider' and The Prodigal Son," in *Journal of the Warburg and Courtauld Institutes*, vol. 33 (1970): 292–303.

Campbell 1973. Colin Campbell. "The Identity of Rembrandt's 'Polish Rider,'" in *Neue Beiträge zur Rembrandt-Forschung*. Edited by Otto von Simson and Jan Kelch. Berlin: Mann, 1973.

Chapman 1990. H. Perry Chapman. *Rembrandt's Self-Portraits: A Study in Seventeenth-Century Identity.* Princeton: Princeton University Press, 1990.

Chapman 2005. H. Perry Chapman. "The Imagined Studios of Rembrandt & Vermeer," in *Inventions of the Studio: Renaissance to Romanticism*. Edited by Michael Cole and Mary Pardo. Chapel Hill and London: University of North Carolina Press, 2005.

Chapman 2008. H. Perry Chapman. "Rembrandt, Van Gogh: Rivalry and Emulation," in *Rembrandt: Three Faces of the Master*, exh. cat. Edited by Benedict Leca. Cincinnati: Cincinnati Art Museum, 2008.

Chapman and Woodall 2010. H. Perry Chapman and Joanna Woodall. "Introduction: The Netherlander has intelligence in his hand," in *Envisioning the Artist in the Early Modern Netherlands*. Edited by H. Perry Chapman and Joanna Woodall. Zwolle: Waanders, 2010.

Chong 2001. Alan Chong. "The Myth of Young Genius: Understanding Rembrandt's Early Career" in *Rembrandt Creates Rembrandt: Art and Ambition in Leiden, 1629–1631*, exh. cat. Boston: Isabella Stewart Gardner Museum, 2001.

Chrościcki 1981. Juliusz A. Chrościcki. "Rembrandt's Polish Rider: Allegory or Portrait?," in *Ars Auro Prior. Studia Ioanni Białostocki Sexagenario Dicata.* Warsaw: Państwowe Wydawnictwo Naukowe, 1981.

Ciechanowiecki 1960. Andrew Ciechanowiecki. "Notes on the Ownership of Rembrandt's Polish Rider," in *The Art Bulletin*, vol. 42, no. 4 (December 1960): 294–96.

Clark 1966. Kenneth Clark. *Rembrandt and the Italian Renaissance.* New York: New York University Press, 1966.

Clark 1978. Kenneth Clark. *An Introduction to Rembrandt.* London: J. Murray, 1978.

Collins-Baker n.d. C.H. Collins-Baker, ed. *The Art Treasures of Great Britain, Part One.* London and Toronto: J. M. Dent and Sons Limited, n.d. [1915?].

Cómez Ramos 1999. Rafael Cómez Ramos. "El 'Ex-Jinete Polaco' de Rembrandt: Una Nueva Lectura," in *Laboratoria de Arte*, vol. 12 (1999): 135–42.

Condon, Cohn, and Mongan 1983–84. Patricia Condon with Marjorie B. Cohn and Agnes Mongan. *In Pursuit of Perfection: The Art of J.-A.-D. Ingres*, exh. cat. Louisville: J.B. Speed Art Museum; Fort Worth: Kimbell Art Museum, 1983–84.

Corpus 1982. Josua Bruyn, et al. *A Corpus of Rembrandt Paintings*, vol. 1. Stichting Foundation Rembrandt Research Project. Dordrecht: Nijhoff, 1982.

Corpus 1986. Josua Bruyn, et al. *A Corpus of Rembrandt Paintings*, vol. 2. Stichting Foundation Rembrandt Research Project. Dordrecht: Nijhoff, 1986.

Corpus 2005. Ernst van de Wetering, et al. *A Corpus of Rembrandt Paintings, Vol. 4: The Self-Portraits.* Stichting Foundation Rembrandt Research Project. The Hague: M. Nijhoff Publishers, 2005.

Corpus 2010. Ernst van de Wetering, et al. *A Corpus of Rembrandt, Vol. 5: The Small-Scale History Paintings.* Stichting Foundation Rembrandt Research Project. Heidelberg: Springer Verlag, 2010.

Cox 1909. Kenyon Cox. "Dutch Paintings in the Hudson-Fulton Exhibition," in *The Burlington Magazine*, vol. 16, no. 81 (December 1909): 178–79 and 183–84.

Crenshaw 2006. Paul Crenshaw. *Rembrandt's Bankruptcy*. New York: Cambridge University Press, 2006.

Danto 1974. Arthur C. Danto. "The Transfiguration of the Commonplace," in *The Journal of Aesthetics and Art Criticism*, vol. 33, no. 2 (Winter 1974): 139–48.

De Coo 1975. Jozef de Coo. "Die bemalten Holzteller, bekannte und neuentdeckte: ihr Schmuck und seine Herkunft," in *Wallraff-Richartz-Jahrbuch*, vol. 37 (1975): 85–118.

De Vries 1978. A. B. de Vries, et al. *Rembrandt in the Mauritshuis*. Alphen aan de Rijn: Sijthoff & Hoordhoff, 1978.

De Winkel 2006. Marieke de Winkel. *Fashion and Fancy: Dress and Meaning in Rembrandt's Paintings*. Amsterdam: Amsterdam University Press, 2006.

Deyell 1980. Daniel Wayne Deyell. "The Frick Collection *Rider* by Rembrandt van Rijn." M.A. thesis, University of British Columbia, 1980.

Dickey 2004. Stephanie Dickey. *Rembrandt: Portraits in Print*. Amsterdam and Philadelphia: John Benjamins Publishing Company, 2004.

Dilworth 2000. Thomas Dilworth. "Letters from David Jones to Kenneth Clark," in *The Burlington Magazine*, vol. 142, no. 1165 (April 2000): 215–25.

Dudok van Heel 2006. S.A.C. Dudok van Heel. *De Jonge Rembrandt onder Tijdgenoten: Godsdienst en Schilderkunst in Leiden en Amsterdam*. Rotterdam: Veenman, 2006.

Dutuit 1885. Eugène Dutuit. *Tableaux et dessins de Rembrandt: catalogue historique et descriptif: description de tous les tableaux connus et des dessins du maître existant dans les galeries publiques et privées ou ayant figuré dans des ventes publiques*. Paris: A. Lévy, 1885.

Elias 1903–5. Johan E. Elias. *De Vroedschap van Amsterdam, 1578–1795*. 2 vols. Haarlem: V. Loosjes, 1903–5.

Erpel 1967. Fritz Erpel. *Die Selbstbildnisse Rembrandts*. Berlin: Henschelverlag, 1967.

Friedländer 1926. M.J. Friedländer. *Die niederländischen Maler des 17. Jahrhunderts*. Berlin: Im Propyläen-Verlag, 1926.

Fuchs 1968. Rudolf Herman Fuchs. *Rembrandt en Amsterdam*. Rotterdam: Lemniscaat, 1968.

Fullerton 1982. Peter Fullerton. "Patronage and Pedagogy: The British Institution in the Early Nineteenth Century," in *Art History*, vol. 5, no. 1 (March 1982): 59–72.

Galassi 2000. Susan Grace Galassi. "Henry Clay Frick as a Collector of Drawings and Later Additions to the Frick Collection," in *Master Drawings*, vol. 38, no 3 (autumn 2000): 285–92.

Gerson 1956. Horst Gerson. "Rembrandt in Poland," in *The Burlington Magazine*, vol. 98, no. 641 (August 1956): 280–83.

Gerson 1968. Horst Gerson. *Rembrandt Paintings*. New York: Reynal, 1968.

Gerson 1969. Horst Gerson, revision of Abraham Bredius 1935. *Rembrandt: The Complete Edition of Paintings*. London and New York: Phaidon, 1969.

Gerson 1971. Horst Gerson, revision of Abraham Bredius 1935. *Rembrandt: The Complete Edition of Paintings*. London and New York: Phaidon, 1971.

Gimpel 1966. René Gimpel. *Diary of an Art Dealer*. New York: Farrar, Straus and Giroux, 1966.

Goldscheider 1960. Ludwig Goldscheider. *Rembrandt: Paintings, Drawings, and Etchings: The Three Early Biographies*. London: Phaidon, 1960.

Gregorovich 2007. Andrew Gregorovich. "Rembrandt's Painting *Cossack Rider*," in *Forum: A Ukrainian Review*, no. 114 (fall/winter 2007): 5–10.

Haak 1969. Bob Haak. *Rembrandt: His Life, Work and Times*. New York: Abrams, 1969.

Hadley 1987. Rollin van N. Hadley, ed. *The Letters of Bernard Berenson and Isabella Stewart Gardner, with Correspondence by Mary Berenson*. Boston: Northeastern University Press, 1987.

Hall 1911. "Art, Music, and Drama: The Art of 1910," in *Hazell's Annual for 1911: A Record of the Men and Movements of the Time*. Edited by Hammond Hall. London: Hazell, Watson, & Viney, 1911.

Hall 1992. Nicholas Hall. *Colnaghi in America*. New York: Colnaghi, 1992.

Hamann 1948. Richard Hamann. *Rembrandt*. Potsdam: Eduard Stichnote, 1948.

Hanfstaengl 1949. Eberhard Hanfstaengl. *Rembrandt Harmensz. van Rijn*. Munich: Münchner Verlag und Graphische Kunstanstalten, 1949.

Harvey 1928. George Harvey. *Henry Clay Frick. The Man*. New York and London: C. Scribner's Sons, 1928.

Haskell 2000. Francis Haskell. *The Ephemeral Museum: Old Master Paintings and the Rise of the Art Exhibition*. New Haven and London: Yale University Press, 2000.

Haussherr 1976. Reiner Haussherr. *Rembrandts Jacobssegen: Überlegungen zur Deutung d. Gemäldes in d. Kasseler Galerie*. Opladen: Westdeutscher Verlag, 1976.

Haverkamp-Begemann 1971. Egbert Haverkamp-Begemann. "The Present State of Rembrandt Studies," in *The Art Bulletin*, vol. 53, no. 1 (March 1971): 88–104.

Held 1944. Julius Held. "Rembrandt's 'Polish' Rider," in *The Art Bulletin*, vol. 26 (December 1944): 246–65.

Held 1969. Julius Held. "The 'Polish' Rider," in *Rembrandt Studies*. Princeton: Princeton University Press, 1969.

Held 1991. Julius Held. "The 'Polish' Rider Revisited: Postscript," in *Rembrandt Studies*. Revised and expanded edition. Princeton: Princeton University Press, 1991.

Hind 1932. Arthur M. Hind. *Rembrandt*. Cambridge, Massachusetts: Harvard University Press, 1932.

Hinterding 2006. Erik Hinterding. *Rembrandt as an Etcher*. Ouderkerk aan den Ijssel: Sound & Vision, 2006.

Hinterding 2008. Erik Hinterding. *Rembrandt Etchings from the Frits Lugt Collection*. Bussum: Thoth Publishers; Paris: Fondation Custodia, 2008.

Hinterding and Horsch 1989. Erik Hinterding and Femy Horsch, "'A Small but Choice Collection': The Art Gallery of King Willem II of the Netherlands (1792–1849)," in *Simiolus*, vol. 19, no. 1–2 (1989): 4–122.

Hochfield 1987. Sylvia Hochfield. "Rembrandt and the Unvarnished Truth," in *Art News*, vol. 86 (December 1987): 102–11.

Hofstede de Groot 1898. Cornelis Hofstede de Groot. *De Rembrandt Tentoonstelling te Amsterdam*. Amsterdam: Scheltema & Holkema's Boekhandel, 1898.

Hofstede de Groot 1906. Cornelis Hofstede de Groot. *Die Urkunden über Rembrandt*. The Hague: M. Nijhoff, 1906.

Hofstede de Groot 1915. Cornelis Hofstede de Groot. *Beschreibendes und kritisches Verzeichnis der Werke der hervorragendsten holländischen Maler des XVII. Jahrhunderts*, vol. 6. Esslingen: P. Neff, 1915.

Hofstede de Groot 1916. Cornelis Hofstede de Groot. *A Catalogue Raisonné of the Works of the Dutch Painters*, vol. 6. Translated by E. Hawke. London: Macmillan, 1916.

Holman 1910. Louis A. Holman. "America's Rembrandts: Remarkable Increase in American Purchases of Paintings by the Dutch Master, with a List of Canvases Owned in the United States and Canada," in *The Century Magazine* (1910): 881–87.

Holmes 1908. Charles John Holmes. "Rembrandt and Van Dyck in the Widener and Frick Collections," in *The Burlington Magazine*, vol. 13, no. 65 (August 1908): 306–16.

Holmes 1911. Charles John Holmes. *Notes on the Art of Rembrandt*, London: Chatto & Windus, 1911.

Hoving 1984. Thomas Hoving. "How Many Sublime Works of Art Are There in American Public Collections?," in *The Connoisseur* (July 1984): 44–45.

Howard 2010. Jeremy Howard. "A Masterly Old Master Dealer of the Gilded Age: Otto Gutekunst and Colnaghi," in *Colnaghi. Established 1760. The History*. Edited by Jeremy Howard. London: Colnaghi, 2010.

Janas and Wójcik 1994. Aleksandra Janas and Adam Wójcik. *Zamek Tarnowskich W Dzikowie*. Tarnobrzeg, Poland: Museum Historyczne Miasta Tarnobrzega, 1994.

Kannegieter 1970. J. Z. Kannegieter. "De Poolse Ruiter, deel 2," in *Kroniek van het Rembrandthuis*, vol. 24 (1970): 85–88.

Kitson 1982. Michael Kitson. *Rembrandt*. Oxford: Phaidon, 1982.

Koning 1986. Hans Koning. "The Real Rembrandt," in *The Connoisseur* (1986): 106.

Korteweg 2006. Anne S. Korteweg. *Guide to the French-Language Medieval Manuscripts in the Koninklijke Bibliotheek*. Amsterdam: Moran Micropublications, 2006.

Krempel 2005. Léon Krempel. *Holländische Gemälde im Städel, 1550–1800*, vol. 2: *Künstler geboren 1615 bis 1630*. Frankfurt am Main and Petersberg: Michael Imhof Verlag, 2005.

Lammertse 2006. Friso Lammertse. *Uylenburgh & Son: Art and Commerce from Rembrandt to De Lairesse, 1625–1675*. Zwolle: Waanders, 2006.

Le Bot 1990. Marc Le Bot. *Rembrandt et l'Orient*. Paris: Flammarion, 1990.

Lecaldano 1969. Paolo Lecaldano. *The Complete Paintings of Rembrandt*. New York: Abrams, 1969.

Liedtke 1992. Walter Liedtke. "Rembrandt and the Rembrandt Style," in *Apollo*, vol. 135, no. 361 (March 1992): 140–45.

Liedtke 1995. Walter Liedtke, et al. *Rembrandt/Not Rembrandt in The Metropolitan Museum of Art: Aspects of Connoisseurship*, vol. 2. New York: The Metropolitan Museum of Art, 1995.

Liedtke 2007. Walter Liedtke. *Dutch Paintings in The Metropolitan Museum of Art*. New York: The Metropolitan Museum of Art, 2007.

London 1815. *Pictures by Rubens, Rembrandt, VanDyke [sic], and Other Artists of the Flemish and Dutch Schools*, exh. cat. London: British Institution, 1815.

London 1853. *Catalogue of Pictures by Italian, Spanish, Flemish, Dutch, French and English Masters*, exh. cat. London: British Institution, 1853.

London 1876. "The Private Collections of England: No. XXVIII.–Castle Howard: Low Country Schools," in *The Athenaeum*, no. 2554 (October 7, 1876): 468–70.

London 1883. *Catalogue of Pictures Belonging to the Earl of Ilchester*. London: privately printed, 1883.

London 1889. *Exhibition of Works by Old Masters and by Deceased Masters of the British School: Winter Exhibition*, exh. cat. London: Royal Academy, 1889.

London 1899. *Works by Rembrandt: Winter Exhibition*, exh. cat. London: Royal Academy, 1899.

London 1903. *Old Masters Exhibition*, exh. cat. London: Royal Academy, 1903.

London 1907. *Original Drawings by Rembrandt in the Collection of J.P.H.* London: Chiswick Press, 1907.

Lorentz 1956. Stanisław Lorentz. *Museums and Collections in Poland, 1945–1955*. Warsaw: Polonia Publishing House, 1956.

Los Angeles 2009–10. Holm Bevers, Lee Hendrix, William Robinson, and Peter Schatborn. *Drawings by Rembrandt and His Pupils: Telling the Difference*, exh. cat. Los Angeles: J. Paul Getty Museum, 2009–10.

Lotus 1910. "Mr. Frick's Rembrandt (F. Warren Cornish on 'The Polish Rider' in the Spectator)," in *The Lotus Magazine*, vol. 1, no. 8 (1910): 7–8.

Lowenthal 1981. Anne W. Lowenthal. *Rembrandt van Rijn*. Mount Vernon, New York: Artist's Limited Edition, 1981.

Lugt 1915. Frits Lugt. *Rembrandt's Amsterdam*. Boston: Museum of Fine Arts, 1915, p. 162.

Lugt 1943. Frits Lugt. "History of Art," in *The Contribution of Holland to the Sciences*. Adriaan Jacob Barnouw, ed. New York: Querido, 1943.

Luijten 1999. Ger Luijten. "The *Iconography:* Van Dyck's Portraits in Print," in *Anthony van Dyck as a Printmaker*, exh. cat. Amsterdam: Rijksmuseum, 1999.

Martin 1921. Wilhelm Martin. "Rembrandt-Rätsel (II)," in *Der Kunstwanderer*, vol. 3 (1921): 30–34.

Martin 1936. Wilhelm Martin. *Rembrandt en zijn tijd*. Amsterdam: J.M. Meulenhoff, 1936.

Martin 1948. Wilhelm Martin. *Rembrandt Gemälde*. Zurich: Fretz und Wasmuth Verlag, 1948.

Massar 1968. Phyllis D. Massar. "Presenting Stefano della Bella," in *The Metropolitan Museum of Art Bulletin*, vol. 27, no. 3 (November 1968): 159–76.

Meldrum 1922/23. David Storrar Meldrum. *Rembrandt's Paintings with an Essay on his Life and Work*. New York: E.P. Dutton, 1922/23.

Michel 1893. Émile Michel. *Rembrandt: Sa vie, son oeuvre, et son temps*. 2 vols. Paris: Hachette, 1893.

Michel 1894. Émile Michel. *Rembrandt: His Life, His Work, and His Time*. 2 vols. Translated by Florence Simmonds. New York: C. Scribner's Sons, 1894.

Miller 1985. Jonathan Miller. "The Mind's Eye and the Human Eye," in *Daedalus*, vol. 114, no. 4 (fall 1985): 185–89.

Minty 2003. Nancy T. Minty. "Dutch and Flemish Seventeenth-Century Art in America, 1800–1940: Collections, Connoisseurship and Perceptions." Ph. D. dissertation, Institute of Fine Arts, New York University, 2003.

Moes 1905. Ernst Wilhelm Moes. *Iconographia Batava*. 2 vols. Amsterdam: Frederik Muller & Co., 1905.

Müller Hofstede 1963. Cornelius Müller Hofstede. "Das Stuttgartner Selbstbildnis von Rembrandt," in *Pantheon*, no. 2 (1963): 65–90.

Munhall 1988. Edgar Munhall, et al. *Henry Clay Frick, the Young Collector*, exh. cat. New York: The Frick Collection, 1988.

Munhall and Grier 1970. Edgar Munhall. *Masterpieces of The Frick Collection*. Introduction by Harry D. M. Grier. New York: The Frick Collection, 1970.

New York 1812. *Catalogue of M. Paff's Gallery of Paintings. No. 221, Broadway. Opposite the Park*. New York, May 15, 1812.

New York 1908a. *An Exhibition of Paintings from the Collection of Mr. Henry C. Frick*, exh. cat. New York: The Union League Club, 1908.

New York 1908b. *Catalogue of the Henry C. Frick Collection of Paintings*. New York: The Frick Collection, 1908.

New York 1913. *Notable Paintings by Great Masters Belonging to the Estate of the Late M.C.D. Borden, Esq.* New York: American Art Association, February 13–14, 1913.

New York 1951. *The Frick Collection, Volume IV: Drawings and Prints.* Edited by David Jacques Way. New York: Frick Art Reference Library, 1951.

New York 1968. *The Frick Collection: An Illustrated Catalogue,* vol. 1, *American, British, Dutch, Flemish, and German Paintings.* Princeton: Princeton University Press, 1968.

New York 1990. *Paintings from The Frick Collection.* New York: Harry N. Abrams, 1990.

New York 1993. *Splendid Legacy: The Havemeyer Collection,* exh cat. New York: The Metropolitan Museum of Art, 1993.

New York 1996. *Art in The Frick Collection.* New York: Harry N. Abrams, 1996.

New York 1998. *Fifteenth- to Eighteenth-Century European Paintings in the Robert Lehman Collection.* New York: The Metropolitan Museum of Art, 1998.

New York 2003. *The Frick Collection: An Illustrated Catalogue,* vol. IX, *Drawings, Prints, and Later Acquisitions.* Princeton: Princeton University Press, 2003.

New York 2004a. *The Frick Collection: Handbook of Paintings.* New York: Scala Publishers, 2004.

New York 2004b. *The Frick Collection: A Tour.* New York: Scala Publishers, 2004.

Nicolle 1898. Marcel Nicolle. "L'Exposition Rembrandt à Amsterdam – II," in *La Revue de l'Art Ancien et Moderne* (December 1898).

Nieuwenhuys 1843. C. J. Nieuwenhuys. *Description de la Galerie des Tableaux de S.M. Le Roi des Pays-Bas.* Brussels: Delavingne et Callewaert, 1843.

Pächt 1991. Otto Pächt. *Rembrandt.* Munich: Prestel, 1991.

Paris 1766. Pierre Remy. *Catalogue raisonné de tableaux de differens bons maîtres des trois écoles, de figures, bustes & autres ouvrage de bronze & de marbre, de porcelaines, & autres effets qui composent le Cabinet de feu M. Aved, Peintre du Roi & de son Académie.* November 24, 1766, Paris.

Paris 1897. *Catalogue de l'exposition des portraits de femmes et d'enfants: ouverte au profit de l'œuvre à l'École des beaux-arts: 30 avril 1897,* exh. cat. Paris: Société philanthropique, 1897.

Paris 1994. *Collection Frits Lugt.* Paris: Fondation Custodia, 1994.

Pinder 1950. Wilhem Pinder. *Rembrandts Selbstbildnisse.* Königstein im Taunus: K. R. Langewiesche, 1950.

Pittsburgh 1949. *The Frick Collection: An Illustrated Catalogue of the Works of Art in the Collection of Henry Clay Frick,* vol. 1. Edited by Mortimer Clapp. Pittsburgh: University of Pittsburgh, 1949.

Potterton 1986. Homan Potterton. *Dutch Seventeenth and Eighteenth Century Paintings in the National Gallery of Ireland. A Complete Catalogue.* Dublin: The National Gallery of Ireland, 1986.

Quick 1985. Jonathan R. Quick. "Virginia Woolf, Roger Fry, and Post-Impressionism," in *The Massachusetts Review,* vol. 26, no. 4 (winter 1985): 547–70.

Quodbach 2004–5. Esmée Quodbach. "Rembrandt's 'Gilder' Is Here: How America Got Its First Rembrandt and France Lost Many of Its Old Masters," in *Simiolus,* vol. 31, no. 1/2 (2004–5): 90–107.

Quodbach 2009. Esmée Quodbach. "'I want this collection to be my monument': Henry Clay Frick and the Formation of The Frick Collection," in *Journal of the History of Collecting,* vol. 21, no. 2 (2009): 229–40.

Reitsma 1997. Ella Reitsma. "Frits Lugt: A Boy with a Vocation" in *Rembrandt: A Biography by Frits Lugt 1899.* Paris: Fondation Custodia, 1997.

Reitsma 2002. Ella Reitsma. "Frits Lugt, a Collector with a Mission" in Quentin Buvelot and Hans Buijs. *A Choice Collection: Seventeenth-Century Dutch Paintings from the Frits Lugt Collection.* The Hague: Royal Cabinet of Paintings; Mauritshuis; Zwolle: Waanders, 2002.

Reitsma and Ponsen 2001. H. J. Reitsma and Arti Ponsen. "The Leiden Disaster of 1807," in *International Journal of Impact Engineering,* vol. 25, no. 5 (May 2001): 507–14.

Rheims 1969. Maurice Rheims. "Rembrandt: Les Destins de ses tableaux," in *Jardin des Arts,* no. 176–77 (July–August 1969): 42–47.

Roberts 1912. William Roberts. "Mr. H. C. Frick's Collection of Pictures," in *The Connoisseur* (November 1912): 147–58.

Roberts 1972. Keith Roberts. "Frick, Gulbenkian & Co," in *The Burlington Magazine,* vol. 114, no. 831 (June 1972): 405–409.

Rosand 2000. David Rosand. "Titian's Dutch Disciple," in *Rembrandt and the Venetian Influence*, exh. cat. New York: Salander-O'Reilly Galleries, 2000.

Roscam Abbing 1987. Michiel Roscam Abbing. *Van Hoogstraten: Iconografie van een familie*. Amsterdam: 1987.

Roscam Abbing 1989. Michiel Roscam Abbing. "Jan van Hoogstraten: leerling van Rembrandt," in *Kroniek van het Rembrandthuis*, vol. 41, no. 1 (1989): 2–18.

Rosenberg 1948. Jakob Rosenberg. *Rembrandt*. 2 vols. Cambridge, Massachusetts: Harvard University Press, 1948.

Rosenberg 1964. Jakob Rosenberg. *Rembrandt: Life and Work*. London: Phaidon, 1964.

Rotterdam 1956. *Rembrandt, 1606–1956: tekeningen: Tentoonstelling ter herdenking van de geboorte van Rembrandt op 15 Juli 1606*, exh. cat. Rotterdam: Museum Boijmans Van Beuningen; Amsterdam: Rijksmuseum, 1956.

Salomon 2010. Xavier F. Salomon. *Masterpieces of European Painting from Dulwich Picture Gallery*, exh. cat. New York: The Frick Collection, 2010.

Saltzman 2008. Cynthia Saltzman. *Old Masters, New World: America's Raid on Europe's Great Pictures 1880–World War I*. London and New York: Viking, 2008.

Saltzman 2010. Cynthia Saltzman. "The Finest Things: Colnaghi, Knoedler and Henry Clay Frick," in *Colnaghi. Established 1760. The History*. Edited by Jeremy Howard. London: Colnaghi, 2010.

Sanger 1998. Martha Frick Symington Sanger. *Henry Clay Frick: An Intimate Portrait*. New York: Abbeville Press Publishers, 1998.

Scallen 1998. Catherine Scallen. "Rembrandt, Emulation, and the Northern Print Tradition," in *In Detail: New Studies of Northern Renaissance Art in Honor of Walter S. Gibson*. Edited by Laurinda S. Dixon. Turnhout: Brepols, 1998.

Scallen 2004. Catherine Scallen. *Rembrandt, Reputation, and the Practice of Connoisseurship*. Amsterdam: Amsterdam University Press, 2004.

Schama 1999. Simon Schama. *Rembrandt's Eyes*. New York: Alfred A. Knopf, 1999.

Schatborn 1998. Peter Schatborn. "Pantalone as New Yorker: Rembrandt and R. B. Kitaj," in *Master Drawings*, vol. 36, no. 1 (Spring 1998): 66–73.

Schatborn 2010. Peter Schatborn. *Rembrandt and His Circle. Drawings in the Frits Lugt Collection*. Bussum: Uitgeverij Thoth, 2010.

Scheltema 1817. Jacobus Scheltema. *Rusland en de Nederlanden*. 4 vols. Amsterdam: Hendrik Gartman, 1817.

Scheurleer 1956. Theodoor Herman Lunsingh Scheurleer. "Rembrandt in het Rijksmuseum," in *Bulletin van het Rijksmuseum*, vol. 4, no. 2 (1956): 27–41.

Schwartz 1984. Gary Schwartz. *Rembrandt: Zijn Leven, Zijn Schilderijen*. Maarsen: 1984.

Schwartz 1985. Gary Schwartz. *Rembrandt: His Life, His Paintings*. New York: Viking, 1985.

Schwartz 2006. Gary Schwartz. *Rembrandt's Universe: His Art, His Life, His World*. London: Thames & Hudson, 2006.

Sedelmeyer 1898. Charles Sedelmeyer. *Illustrated catalogue of 300 paintings by old masters of the Dutch, Flemish, Italian, French, and English schools, being some of the principal pictures which have at various times formed part of the Sedelmeyer Gallery*. Paris: Printed for Charles Sedelmeyer by Lahure, 1898.

Sickert 1947. Walter Sickert. *A Free House: Or the Artist as Craftsman*. London: Macmillan, 1947.

Siple 1936. Ella S. Siple. "The Opening of the Frick Collection," in *The Burlington Magazine*, vol. 68, no. 395 (February, 1936): 102–3.

Sitwell 1947. Osbert Sitwell, ed. *A Free House! Or the Artist as Craftsman. Being the Writings of Walter Richard Sickert*. London: Macmillan & Co., 1947.

Slatkes 1983. Leonard Slatkes. *Rembrandt and Persia*. New York: Abaris Books, 1983.

Slatkes 1989. Leonard Slatkes. "Review of *Rembrandt Research Project, A Corpus of Rembrandt Paintings*," in *The Art Bulletin*, vol. 71, no. 1 (March 1989): 139–44.

Slatkes 1992. Leonard J. Slatkes. *Rembrandt: Catalogo completo dei dipinti*. Florence: Cantini, 1992.

Slive 1970–74. Seymour Slive. *Frans Hals* (3 vols). London: Phaidon, 1970–74.

Slive 2009. Seymour Slive. *Rembrandt Drawings*. Los Angeles: J. Paul Getty Museum, 2009

Sluijter 2000. Eric Jan Sluijter. *Seductress of Sight: Studies in Dutch Art of the Golden Age*. Zwolle: Waanders, 2000.

Sluijter 2006. Eric Jan Sluijter. *Rembrandt and the Female Nude* Amsterdam: Amsterdam University Press, 2006.

Smith 1836. John Smith. *Catalogue Raisonné of the Works of the Most Eminent Dutch, Flemish, and French Painters*, vol. 7. London: Smith and Son, 1836.

Solkin 1999. David Solkin. "Isaac Fuller's Escape of Charles II: A Restoration Tragicomedy," in *Journal of the Warburg and Courtauld Institutes*, vol. 62 (1999): 199–240.

Stansky 1996. Peter Stansky. *On or About December 1910: Early Bloomsbury and Its Intimate World*. Cambridge and London: Harvard University Press, 1996.

Stowe 1854. Harriet Beecher Stowe. *Sunny Memories of Foreign Lands*. London: G. Routledge & Co., 1854.

Straten 2005. Roelof van Straten. *Young Rembrandt: The Leiden Years, 1606–1632*. Leiden: Foleor, 2005.

Strauss and van der Meulen 1979. Walter L. Strauss and Marjon van der Meulen, eds. *The Rembrandt Documents*. New York: Abaris Books, 1979.

Sumowski 1983. Werner Sumowski. *Gemälde der Rembrandt-Schüler*. 6 vols. Landau: Edition PVA, 1983 [–1994].

Sutton 1972. Denys Sutton, ed. *Letters of Roger Fry*, vol. 1. London: Chatto and Windus, 1972.

Sutton 1985. Denys Sutton. "Herbert Horne and Roger Fry," in *Apollo*, vol. 122, no. 282 (August 1985): 130–59.

Tatham 1811. Charles Heathcote Tatham. *The Gallery at Castle Howard, in Yorkshire; the Seat of the Earl of Carlisle*. London: printed for T. Gardiner, Princes-Street, Cavendish-Square; and Longman, Hurst, Rees, Orme, and Brown, Paternoster-Row; by J. Barfield, Wardour, 1811.

Thieme-Becker 1933. Ulrich Thieme and Felix Becker, eds. *Allgemeines Lexikon der bildenden Künstler von der Antike bis zur Gegenwart: unter Mitwirkung von 300 Fachgelehrten des In- und Auslandes*, vol. 27. Leipzig: E. A. Seemann, 1933.

Thieme-Becker 1942. Ulrich Thieme and Felix Becker, eds. *Allgemeines Lexikon der bildenden Künstler von der Antike bis zur Gegenwart: unter Mitwirkung von 300 Fachgelehrten des In- und Auslandes*, vol. 35, Leipzig: E. A. Seemann, 1942.

Tümpel 1986. Christian Tümpel. *Rembrandt: Mythos und Methode*, Königstein im Taunus: Langewiesche, 1986.

Tümpel 1993. Christian and Astrid Tümpel. *Rembrandt: All Paintings in Colour*. Antwerp: Fonds Mercator, 1993.

Valentiner 1908. Wilhelm R. Valentiner. *Rembrandt: Des Meisters Gemälde in 643 Abbildungen* (Klassiker der Kunst). Stuttgart: Deutsche Verlags-Anstalt, 1908.

Valentiner 1909. Wilhelm R. Valentiner. *The Hudson-Fulton Celebration*, vol. 2: *Catalogue of a Collection of Paintings by Dutch Masters of the Seventeenth Century*, exh. cat. New York: The Metropolitan Museum of Art, 1909.

Valentiner 1914. Wilhelm R. Valentiner. "Zur Benennung einiger Bildnisse Rembrandts," in *Monatshefte für Kunstwissenschaft* (1914): 279–82.

Valentiner 1921. Wilhelm R. Valentiner. *Rembrandt Wiedergefundene Gemälde (1910–1920) in 120 Abbildungen*. Stuttgart and Berlin: Deutsche Verlags-Anstalt, 1921.

Valentiner 1921. Wilhelm R. Valentiner. *The Work of Rembrandt*. Third edition. Introduction by Adolf Rosenberg. New York: Brentano's, 1921.

Valentiner 1930. Wilhelm R. Valentiner. "Important Rembrandts in American Collections," in *Art News*, vol. 28, no. 30 (April 26, 1930): 3–4.

Valentiner 1931. Wilhelm R. Valentiner. *Rembrandt Paintings in America*. New York: S. W. Frankel, 1931.

Valentiner 1932. Wilhelm R. Valentiner. "Carel and Barent Fabritius," in *The Art Bulletin*, vol. 14, no. 3 (Sept. 1932): 197–241.

Valentiner 1941. Wilhelm R. Valentiner. "Jan van de Cappelle," in *Art Quarterly* (Autumn 1941): 272–96.

Valentiner 1948. Wilhelm R. Valentiner. "Rembrandt's Conception of Historical Portraiture," in *Art Quarterly*, vol. 11, no. 2 (Spring 1948): 117–35.

Van Bemmelen 1929. J. F. van Bemmelen. "Identificatie van Familie-portretten," in *Jaarboek van het Genootschap Amstelodamum*, vol. 26 (1929): 59–77.

Van Berge-Gerbaud 1997. Mària van Berge-Gerbaud. *Rembrandt et son école: Dessins de la Collection Frits Lugt*. Paris: Fondation Custodia, 1997.

Van de Wetering 2001. Ernst van de Wetering. "Thirty Years of the Rembrandt Research Project," in *IFAR Journal: International Foundation for Art Research*, vol 4, no. 2 (2001): 14–24.

Van de Wetering 2009. Ernst van de Wetering. *Rembrandt: The Painter at Work*. Revised edition. Amsterdam: Amsterdam University Press, 2009.

Van Dyke 1923. John Charles Van Dyke. *Rembrandt and His School; a critical study of the master and his pupils with a new assignment of their pictures.* New York: C. Scribner's Sons, 1923.

Van Eeghen 1977a. Isabella Henriette van Eeghen. "Willem Jansz van der Pluym en Rembrandt," in *Amstelodamum*, vol. 64 (1977): 6–13.

Van Eeghen 1977b. Isabella Henriette van Eeghen. "Voor wie Schilderde Rembrandt het Portret van Nicolaas Ruts," in *Amstelodamum*, vol. 64 (1977): 97–101.

Van Gelder 1940. Hendrik Enno van Gelder. *Rembrandt en zijn tijd.* Amsterdam: H.J.W. Becht, c. 1940.

Van Gelder 1948. Hendrik Enno van Gelder. *Rembrandt en Zijn Portret.* Amsterdam: H. J. W. Becht, 1948.

Van Thiel 1992. P. J. J. van Thiel. "De Rembrandt-tentoonstelling van 1898," in *Bulletin van het Rijksmuseum*, vol. 40, no. 1 (1992): 11–93.

Vels Heijn 1989. Annemarie Vels Heijn. *Rembrandt.* Amsterdam: Scala Books, 1989.

Vogelaar and Korevaar 2005. Christiaan Vogelaar and Gerbrand Korevaar, eds. *Rembrandt's Mother: Myth and Reality*, exh. cat. Leiden: Stedelijk Museum De Lakenhal, 2005.

Vosmaer 1877. Carel Vosmaer. *Rembrandt, sa vie et ses oeuvres.* Paris: H. Loones, 1877.

Waagen 1854. Gustav Friedrich Waagen. *Treasures of Art in Great Britain*, vol. 2. London: John Murray, 1854.

Waldmann 1910. Emil Waldmann. "Die Ausstellung holländischer Gemälde des 17. Jahrhunderts in New York," in *Zeitschrift für bildende Kunst* (1910): 73–85.

Ward and Roberts 1907. Thomas Humphry Ward and William Roberts. *Pictures in the Collection of J. Pierpont Morgan at Princes Gate & Dover House, London.* London: privately printed, 1907.

Wardle 1992. Patricia Wardle. "Summaries, The Rembrandt Exhibition of 1898," in *Bulletin van het Rijksmuseum*, vol. 40, no. 1 (1992): 123–27.

Watson 1989. Peter Watson. *Wisdom and Strength: The Biography of a Renaissance Masterpiece.* New York: Doubleday, 1989.

Westermann 2000. Mariët Westermann. *Rembrandt.* London: Phaidon, 2000.

Wheelock 1995. Arthur Wheelock. *Dutch Paintings of the Seventeenth Century.* Washington: National Gallery of Art, 1995.

White 1984. Christopher White. *Rembrandt.* London: Thames and Hudson, 1984.

White 1999. *Rembrandt as an Etcher: A Study of the Artist at Work.* New Haven: Yale University Press, 1999.

White and Buvelot 1999. Christopher White and Quentin Buvelot, eds. *Rembrandt by Himself*, exh. cat. London: National Gallery; The Hague: Mauritshuis, 1999.

Wildenstein 1922. Georges Wildenstein. *Le Peintre Aved:sa vie et son oeuvre 1702–1766*, vol. 1. Paris: Les Beaux-arts, édition d'études et de documents, 1922.

Woolf 1940. Virginia Woolf. *Roger Fry: A Biography.* New York: Harcourt, Brace and Co. 1940.

Wright 1982. Christopher Wright. *Rembrandt: Self-Portraits.* London: G. Fraser, 1982.

Wright 2000. Christopher Wright. *Rembrandt.* Translated by Paul Alexandre. Paris: Citadelles & Mazenod, 2000.

Wurzbach 1906. Alfred von Wurzbach. *Niederländisches Künstler-Lexicon*, vol 1. Vienna: Halm und Goldmann, 1906.

Wurzbach 1910. Alfred von Wurzbach. *Niederländisches Künstler-Lexicon*, vol 2. Vienna: Halm und Goldmann, 1910.

Wurzbach 1911. Alfred von Wurzbach. *Niederländisches Künstler-Lexicon*, vol 3. Vienna: Halm und Goldmann, 1911.

Yourcenar 1957. Marguerite Yourcenar. *Coup de Grâce.* New York: Farrar, Straus and Cudahy, 1957.

Zygas 1999. K. Paul Zygas. "Rembrandt's Lithuanian Rider?," *Lithuanian Heritage*, vol 6, no. 3 (May/June 1999): 6–10 and 31.

Żygulski 1965. Zdzisław Żygulski, Jr. "Rembrandt's 'Lisowcyk': A Study of Costume and Weapons," in *Bulletin du Musée National de Varsovie*, vol 6, no. 2–3 (1965): 43–67.

Żygulski 2000. Zdzisław Żygulski, Jr. "Further Battles for the 'Lisowczyk' (Polish Rider) by Rembrandt," in *Artibus et Historiae*, vol. 21, no. 41 (2000): 197–205.